Goldwin Smith

The Political Destiny of Canada

Goldwin Smith

The Political Destiny of Canada

ISBN/EAN: 9783337069759

Printed in Europe, USA, Canada, Australia, Japan

Cover: Foto ©Suzi / pixelio.de

More available books at **www.hansebooks.com**

THE
POLITICAL DESTINY OF CANADA.

THE POLITICAL DESTINY

OF

CANADA.

BY

GOLDWIN SMITH.

(*Reprinted from* the " *Fortnightly Review.*")

WITH A

REPLY BY SIR FRANCIS HINCKS, K.C.M.G.,

AND

SOME REMARKS **ON THAT** REPLY.

TORONTO:
WILLING & WILLIAMSON.
LONDON:
CHAPMAN & HALL.
1878.

PRINTED AND BOUND
BY
HUNTER, ROSE & CO.,
TORONTO.

PREFACE.

I HAVE reason to believe that some persons would like to have the Essay on the Political Destiny of Canada, which forms the principal part of this volume, and which is reprinted from the *Fortnightly Review*, in a more convenient form than a back number of the periodical in which it appeared. I take the opportunity of replying to some criticisms of Sir Francis Hincks. Sir Francis allows me to insert his paper, so that, if there is any poison in my opinions, the antidote will be found beside the bane.

In the Appendix, are extracts from papers by Mr. Robert Lowe and Lord Blachford, bearing on the subject of my Essay, which I think will repay attention.

At a moment when the mind of the nation is occupied with questions respecting our commercial relations, and our fiscal autonomy, it is surely needless to accumulate arguments for the purpose of proving that wisdom does not prescribe indifference to fundamental problems or blindness to the future.

I write, as I hope and believe, in the interest of the people, English, as well as Canadian. As to the British aristocracy, it has political views of its own in relation to this Continent, which seem to me not consistent with the welfare of those whose lot is cast in the New World.

G. S.

TORONTO, Nov. 1878.

THE POLITICAL DESTINY

OF

CANADA.

IGNORANCE of the future can hardly be good for any man or nation; nor can forecast of the future in the case of any man or nation well interfere with the business of the present, though the language of colonial politicians seems often to imply that it may. No Canadian farmer would take his hand from the plough, no Canadian artisan would desert the foundry or the loom, no Canadian politician would become less busy in his quest of votes, no industry of any kind would slacken, no source of wealth would cease to flow, if the rulers of Canada and the powers of Downing Street, by whom the rulers of Canada are supposed to be guided, instead of drifting on in darkness, knew for what port they were steering.

For those who are actually engaged in moulding the institutions of a young country not to have formed a conception of her destiny—not to have made up their minds whether she is to remain forever a dependency, to blend again in a vast confederation with the monarchy of the mother-country, or to be united to a neighbouring republic—would be to renounce statesmanship. The very expenditure into which Canada is led by her position as a dependency, in military and political railways, in armaments and defences, and other things which assume the permanence of the present system, is enough to convict Canadian rulers of flagrant improvidence if the permanency of the present system is not distinctly established in their minds.

To tax forecast with revolutionary designs or tendencies is absurd. No one can be in a less revolutionary frame of mind than he who foresees a political event without having the slightest interest in hastening its arrival. On the other hand mere party politicians cannot afford to see beyond the hour. Under the system of party government, forecast and freedom of speech alike belong generally to those who are not engaged in public life.

The political destiny of Canada is here considered by itself, apart from that of any other portion of the motley and widely-scattered "empire." This surely is the rational course. Not to speak of India and the military dependencies, such as Malta and Gibraltar, which have absolutely nothing in common with the North American colonies (India not even the titular form of government, since its sovereign has been made an empress), who can believe that the future of Canada, of South Africa, of Australia, of the West Indies, and of Mauritius, will be the same? Who can believe that the mixed French and English population of Canada, the mixed Dutch and English population of the Cape, the negro population of Jamaica, the French and Indian population of Mauritius, the English and Chinese population of Australia, are going to run forever the same political course? Who can believe that the moulding influences will be the same in arctic continents or in tropical islands as in countries lying within the temperate zone? Among the colonies, those, perhaps which most nearly resemble each other in political character and circumstances, are Canada and Australia; yet the elements of the population are very different— and still more different are the external relations of Australia, with no other power near her, from those of Canada, not only conterminous with the United States, but interlaced with them, so that at present the road of the Governor-General of Canada, when he visits his Pacific province, lies through the territory of the American Republic. Is it possible to suppose that the slender filament which connects each of these colonies with Downing Street is the thread of a common destiny?

In studying Canadian politics, and in attempting to cast the political horoscope of Canada, the first thing to be remembered, though official optimism is apt to overlook it, is that Canada was a colony not of England but of France, and that between the British of Ontario and the British of Nova Scotia and New Brunswick are interposed, in solid and unyielding mass, above a million of unassimilated and politically antagonistic Frenchmen. French Canada is a relic of the historical past preserved by isolation, as Siberian mammoths are preserved in ice. It is a fragment of the France before the Revolution, less the monarchy and the aristocracy; for the feeble parody of French feudalism in America ended with the abolition of the seigniories, which may be regarded as the final renunciation of feudal ideas and institutions by society in the New World. The French-Canadians are an unprogressive, religious, submissive, courteous, and, though poor, not unhappy people. They would make excellent factory-hands if Canada had a market for her manufactures; and, perhaps, it is as much due to the climate as to their lack of intelligent industry, that they have a very indifferent reputation as farmers. They are governed by the priest, with the occasional assistance of the notary; and the Roman Catholic Church may be said to be still established in the province, every Roman Catholic being bound to pay tithes and other ecclesiastical imposts, though the Protestant minority are exempt. The Church is immensely rich, and her wealth is always growing, so that the economical element which mingled with the religious causes of the Reformation may one day have its counterpart in Quebec. The French-Canadians, as we have said, retain their exclusive national character. So far from being absorbed by the British population, or Anglicized by contact with it, they have absorbed and Gallicized the fragments of British population which chance has thrown amongst them; and the children of Highland regiments disbanded in Quebec have become thorough Frenchmen, and prefixed Jean Baptiste to their Highland names. For his own Canada the Frenchman of Quebec has something of a patriotic feeling; for France he has filial affection enough to make his heart beat violently for her during a Franco-German war; for England, it may be safely said, he has no feeling whatever. It is true that he fought against the American invaders in the Revolutionary War, and again in 1812; but then he was animated by his ancient hostility to the Puritans of New England, in the factories of whose descendants he now freely seeks employment. Whether he would enthusiastically take up arms for England against the Americans at present, the British War-Office, after the experience of the two Fenian raids, can no doubt tell. With Upper Canada, the land of Scotch Presbyterians, Irish Orangemen, and ultra-British sentiment, French Canada, during the union of the two provinces, led an uneasy life; and she accepted confederation, on terms which leave her nationality untouched, rather as a severance of her special wedlock with her unloved consort than as a measure of North American union The unabated antagonism between the two races and the two religions was plainly manifested on the occasion of the conflict between the French half-breeds and the British immigrants in Manitoba, which presented a faint paralled to the conflict between the advanced posts of slavery and anti-slavery in Kansas on the eve of the civil war; Quebec openly sympathising with Riel and his fellow-insurgents, while Ontario was on fire to avenge the death of Scott. Sir George Cartier might call himself an Englishman speaking French; but his calling himself so did not make him so; much less did it extend the character from a political manager, treading the path of ambition with British colleagues, to the mass of his unsophisticated compatriots. The priests hitherto have put their interests into the hands of a political leader, such as Sir George himself, in the same way in which the Irish priests used to put their interests into the hands of O'Connell; and this leader has made the best terms he could for them and for himself at Ottawa. Nor has it been difficult to make good terms, since both the political parties bid emulously for the Catholic vote, and by their interested subserviency to those who wield it, render it impossible for a Liberal Catholic party, or a Liberal party of any kind, to make head against priestly influence in Quebec. By preference the priests, as reactionists, have allied themselves with the Tory party in the British provinces, and Canada has long witnessed the singular spectacle, witnessed for the first time in England at the last general election, of Roman Catholics and Orangemen marching together to the poll. Fear of contact with an active-minded democracy, and of possible peril to their over-weening wealth, has also led the priesthood to shrink from annexation, though they have not been able to prevent their people from going over the line for better wages, and bringing back with them a certain republican leaven of political and ecclesiastical unrest, which in the end may, perhaps, lead to the verification of Lord Elgin's remark, that it would be easier to make the French Canadians Americans than to make them English. Hitherto, however, French Canada has retained among other heirlooms of the *Ancien Régime*, the old Gallican Church, the Church of Louis XIV. and of Bossuet, national, quiet, unaggressive, capable of living always on sufficiently good terms with the state. But now the scene is changed. Even to French Canada, the most secluded nook of the Catholic world, Ultramontanism has penetrated with the Jesuit in its van. There is a struggle for ascendancy between the Jesuits and the Gallicans, the citadel of the Gallicans being the Sulpician Seminary, vast and enormously wealthy, which rises over Montreal. The Jesuit has the forces of the hour on his side; he gains the day; the bishops fall under his influence, and take his part against the Sulpicians; the Guibord case marks, distinctly though farcically, the triumph of his principles; and it is by no means certain that he, a cosmopolitan power playing a great game, will cling to Canadian isolation, and that he will not prefer a junction with his main army in the United States. Assuredly his choice will not be determined by loyalty to England. At all events, his aggressive policy has begun to raise questions calculated to excite the Protestants of the British provinces, which the politicians, with all their arts, will hardly be able to smother, and which will probably put an end to the long torpor of Quebec. The New Brunswick school case points to education as a subject which can scarcely fail soon to give birth to a cause of war.

Besides the French, there are in Canada, as we believe we have good authority for saying, about 400,000 Irish, whose political sentiments are generally identical with those of the Irish in the mother-country, as any reader of their favourite journals will perceive. Thus, without reckoning a considerable German settlement in Ontario, which by its unimpaired nationality, in the heart of the British population attests the weakness of the assimilating forces in Canada, compared with those in the United States, or the Americans, who, though not numerous, are influential in the commercial centres, we have at once to deduct 1,400,000 from a total population of less than 4,000,000 in order to reduce to reality the pictures of universal devotion to England and English interests which are presented by the speeches of official persons, or of persons professing to know Canada, but deriving their idea of her from the same source.

Confederation, so far, has done nothing to fuse the races, and very little even to unite the provinces. New Brunswick and Nova Scotia, besides being cut off from Ontario by French Canada, have interests of their own, separate, and in some degree divergent, from those of Ontario, New Brunswick especially being drawn by her commercial interests towards New England. The representatives of each of the smaller provinces form a separate group at Ottawa, giving or withholding their support to a great extent from provincial considerations. Each of the two political parties has its base in Ontario, which is the field of the decisive battles; and they can hardly be said to extend to the maritime provinces, much less to Manitoba or to British Columbia. When the Ontarian parties are evenly balanced the smaller provinces turn the scale, and Ontarian Leaders are always buying them with "better terms," that is, alterations of the pecuniary arrangements of confederation in their favour, and other inducements, at the sacrifice, of course, of the general interests of the Confederation. From the composition of a cabinet to the composition of a rifle-team, sectionalism is the rule. Confederation has secured free-trade between the provinces; what other good it has done it would not be easy to say. Whether it has increased the military strength of Canada is a question for the answer to which we must appeal once more to the British War-Office. Canadians have shown, on more than one memorable occasion, that in military spirit they were not wanting; but they cannot be goaded into wasting their hardly-earned money on preparations for a defence which would be hopeless against an invader who will never come. Politically, the proper province of a federal government is the management of external relations, while domestic legislation is the province of the several states. But a dependency has no external relations; Canada has not even, like South Africa, a native question,

B

her Indians being perfectly harmless; and consequently the chief duty of a federal Government in Canada is to keep itself in existence by the ordinary agencies of party, a duty which it discharges with a vengeance. English statesmen bent on extending to all the colonies what they assume to be the benefits of Confederation, should study the Canadian specimen, if possible, on the spot. They will learn, first, that while a spontaneous confederation, such as groups of states have formed under the pressure of a common danger, develops mainly the principles of union, a confederation brought about by external influence is apt to develop the principles of antagonism in at least an equal degree; and secondly, that parliamentary government in a dependency is, to a lamentable extent, government by faction and corruption, and that by superadding federal to provincial government the extent and virulence of those maladies are seriously increased. If an appeal is made to the success of confederation in Switzerland, the answer is, that Switzerland is not a dependency but a nation.

It is of Canada alone that we here speak, and we speak only of her political destiny. The ties of blood, of language, of historical association, and of general sympathy, which bind the British portion of the Canadian people to England, are not dependent on the political connection, nor is it likely that they would be at all weakened by its severance. In the United States there are millions of Irish exiles, with the wrongs of Ireland in their hearts, and the whole nation retains the memories of the Revolutionary War, of the War of 1812, and of the conduct of the British aristocracy towards the United States during the rebellion of the South—conduct which it is difficult to forgive, and which it would be folly to forget. Yet to those who have lived among the Americans it will not seem extravagant to say that the feelings of an Anglo-American towards his mother-country are really at least as warm as those of the natives of dependencies, and at least as likely to be manifested by practical assistance in the hour of need. A reference to the history of the opposition made to the War of 1812, will suffice at least to bring this opinion within the pale of credibility.

The great forces prevail. They prevail at last however numerous and apparently strong the secondary forces opposed to them may be. They prevailed at last in the case of German unity and in the case of Italian independence. In each of those cases the secondary forces were so heavily massed against the event that men renowned for practical wisdom believed the event would never come. It came, irresistible and irreversible, and we now see that Bismarck and Cavour were only the ministers of Fate.

Suspended of course, and long suspended, by the action of the secondary forces, the action of the great forces may be. It was so in both the instances just mentioned. A still more remarkable instance is the long postponement of the union of Scotland with England by the antipathies resulting from the abortive attempt of Edward I., and by a subsequent train of historical accidents, such as the absorption of the energies of England in Continental or civil war. But the union came at last, and, having the great forces on its side, it came forever.

In the case before us, it appears that the great forces are those which make for the political separation of the New from the Old World. They are :—

(1) The distance, which may be shortened by steam and telegraph for the transmission of a despot's commands, but can hardly be much shortened for the purposes of representative government. Steam increases the transatlantic intercourse of the wealthier class, but not that of

the people, who **have neither** money nor time for the passage. **Everything is possible** in the way of nautical invention; **fuel may** be still further economized, though its price is not likely to fall; **but it is** improbable that the **cost of** ship-building or **the** wages of seamen will be reduced; and the growth of manufactures in the New World, which **we** may expect henceforth to be rapid, **can** hardly fail to diminish **the** intercourse dependant on transatlantic trade. A commonwealth spanning the Atlantic may be a grand conception, but political institutions must **after all** bear some relation to Nature **and to** practical convenience. **Few** have fought against geography and prevailed.

2. **Divergence of** interest, which **seems in** this case **to be as wide as** possible. **What** has Canada to do with **the** European **and** Oriental concerns of England, with her European and Oriental diplomacy, with her European and Oriental wars? Can **it** be conceived that Canadian traders would allow their commerce to be cut up by Russian cruisers, or **that** Canadian farmers **would take** arms **and pay war-taxes** in **order to** prevent Russia from obtaining a free passage through the Dardanelles? An English pamphlet called "The **Great Game**" was reprinted the other **day** in Can-

ada; but the chapter on India was omitted, as having no interest for Canadians. For English readers that chapter had probably more interest than all the other chapters put together. On the other hand, whenever a question about boundaries or mutual rights arises with the United States, the English people and the English government betray, by the languor of their diplomacy and the ease with which they yield, their comparative indifference to the objects in which Canada is most concerned. A Canadian periodical some time ago had a remarkable paper by a native writer, showing that the whole series of treaties made by Great Britain with the United States had been a continuous sacrifice of the claims of Canada. It was not, assuredly, that Great Britain wanted either force or spirit to fight for her own rights or interests, but that she felt that Canadian rights and interests were not her own. Her rulers could not have induced her people to go to war for an object for which they cared so little, and had so little reason to care, as a frontier line in North America. Another illustration of the difference between the British and the Canadian point of view was afforded by the recent dispute about the Extradition Treaty. England was disposed to be stiff and punctilious, having comparatively little to fear from the suspension of the treaty; while to Canada, bordering on the United States, the danger was great, and the renewal of the treaty was a vital necessity before which punctiliousness gave way. One object there is connected with the American Continent for which the British aristocracy, if we may judge by the temper it showed and the line it took toward the American Republic at the time of the rebellion, would be not unwilling to run the risk of war. But that object is one with regard to which the interests of British aristocracy and those of Canadian democracy not only are not identical, but point directly opposite ways. With regard to economical questions, the divergence is, if possible, still clearer than with regard to diplomatic questions. The economic interests of Canada must evidently be those of her own continent, and to that continent, by all the economic forces, she must be and visibly is drawn. Her currency, whatever may be the name and superscription on the coin, is American, and it is the sure symbol of her real connection. In the British manufacturer the Canadian manufacturer sees a rival; and Canada at this moment is the scene of a protectionist movement led, curiously enough, by those Conservative politicians who are loudest in their professions of loyalty to Great Britain.

3. More momentous than even the divergence of interest is the divergence of political character, between the citizens of the Old and the citizens of the New World. We speak, of course, not of the French-Canadians, between whom and the people of Great Britain the absence of political affinity is obvious, but of the British communities in North America. The colonization of the New World, at least that English portion of it, which was destined to give birth to the ruling and moulding power, was not merely a migration, but an exodus: it was not merely a local extension of humanity, but a development; it not only peopled another continent, but opened a new era. The curtain rose not for the old drama with fresh actors, but for a fresh drama on a fresh scene. A long farewell was said to feudalism when the New England Colony landed, with the rough draft of a written constitution, which embodied a social compact and founded government not on sacred tradition or divine right, but on reason and the public good. The more one sees of society in the New World, the more convinced one is that its structure essentially differs from that of society in the Old World, and that the feudal element

has been eliminated completely and forever. English aristocracy, fancying itself, as all established systems fancy themselves, the normal and final state of humanity, may cling to the belief that the new development is a mere aberration, and that dire experience will in time bring it back to the ancient path. There are people, it seems, who persuade themselves that America is retrograding towards monarchy and church establishments. No one who knows the Americans can possibly share this dream. Monarchy has found its way to the New World only in the exceptional case of Brazil, to which the royal family of the mother-country itself migrated, and where, after all, the emperor is rather an hereditary president than a monarch of the European type. In Canada, government being parliamentary and "constitutional," monarchy is the delegation of a shadow; and any attempt to convert the shadow into a substance, by introducing a dynasty with a court and civil list, or by reinvesting the viceroy with personal power, would speedily reveal the real nature of the situation. Pitt proposed to extend to Canada what as a Tory minister he necessarily regarded as the blessings of aristocracy; but the plant refused to take root in the alien soil. No peerage ever saw the light in Canada;

the baronetage saw the light and no more; of nobility there is nothing now but a knighthood very small in number, and upon which the Pacific Railway scandal has cast so deep a shadow that the Home Government, though inclined that way, seems shy of venturing on more creations. Hereditary wealth and the custom of primogeniture, indispensable supports of an aristocracy, are totally wanting in a purely industrial country, where, let the law be what it might, natural justice has always protested against the feudal claims of the first-born. To establish in Canada the state Church, which is the grand buttress of aristocracy in England, has proved as hopeless as to establish aristocracy itself. The Church lands have been secularized; the university, once confined to Anglicanism, has been thrown open; the Anglican Church has been reduced to the level of other denominations, though its rulers still cling to the memories and to some relics of their privileged condition. As a religion, Anglicanism has little hold upon the mass of the people; it is recruited by emigration from England, and sustained to a certain extent by a social feeling in its favour among the wealthier class. More democratic churches far exceed it in popularity and propagandist force: Methodism especially, which, in contrast to Episcopacy, sedulously assigns an active part in church-work to every member, decidedly gains ground, and bids fair to become the popular religion of Canada. Nor is the militarism of European aristocracies less alien to industrial Canada than their monarchism and their affinity for state churches. The Canadians, as we have already said, can fight well when real occasion calls; so can their kinsmen across the line; but among the Canadians, as among the people of the Northern States, it is impossible to awaken militarism—every sort of galvanic apparatus has been tried in vain. Distinctions of rank, again, are wanting: everything bespeaks a land dedicated to equality; and fustian, instead of bowing to broadcloth, is rather too apt, by a rude self-assertion, to revenge itself on broadcloth for enforced submissiveness in the old country. Where the relations of classes, the social forces, and the whole spirit of society, are different, the real principles and objects of government will differ also, notwithstanding the formal identity of institutions. It proved impossible, as all careful observers had foreseen, to keep the same political roof over the heads of slavery and antislavery. To keep the same political roof over the heads of British aristocracy and Canadian democracy would be an undertaking only one degree less hopeless. A rupture would come, perhaps, on some question between the ambition of a money-spending nobility and the parsimony of a money-making people. Let aristocracy, hierarchy, and militarism, be content with the Old World; it was conquered by the feudal sword; the New World was conquered only by the axe and plough.

4. The force, sure in the end to be attractive, not repulsive, of the great American community along the edge of which Canada lies, and, to which the British portion of her population is drawn by identity of race, language, religion, and general institutions, the French portion by its connection with the Roman Catholic Church of the States; the whole by economic influences, against which artificial arrangements and sentiments contend in vain, and which are gathering strength and manifesting their ascendancy from hour to hour.

An enumeration of the forces which make in favour of the present connection will show their secondary, and for the most part transient character. The chief of them appear to be these:

a.' The reactionary tendencies of the priesthood which rules French Canada, and which fears that any change might disturb its solitary reign. Strong this force has hitherto been, but its strength depends on isolation, and isolation cannot be permanent. Even the "palæocrystallic" ice which envelops French Canada will melt at last, and when it does, French reaction will be at an end. We have already noted two agencies which are working towards this result—the leaven of American sentiment brought back by French Canadians who have sojourned as artisans in the States, and the ecclesiastical aggressiveness of the Jesuits.

b. "United Empire Loyalism," which has its chief seat in Ontario. Every revolution has its reaction, and in the case of the American Revolution the reaction took the form of a migration of the royalists to Canada, where lands were assigned them, and where they became the political progenitors of the Canadian Tory party, while the "Reformers" are the offspring of a subsequent immigration of Scotch Presbyterians, mingled with wanderers from the United States. The two immigrations were arrayed against each other in 1837, when, though the United Empire Loyalists were victorious in the field, the political victory ultimately rested with the Reformers. United Empire Loyalism is still strong in some districts, while in others the descendants of royalist exiles are found in the ranks of the opposite party. But the whole party is now in the position of the Jacobites after the extinction of the house of Stuart. England has formally recognized the American Revolution, taken part in the celebration of its centenary, and through her ambassador saluted its flag. Anti-revolutionary sentiment ceases to have any meaning, and its death cannot be far off.

c. The influence of English immigrants, especially in the upper ranks of the professions, in the high places of commerce, and in the press. These men have retained a certain social ascendancy; they have valued themselves on their birth in the imperial country and the superior traditions which they supposed it to imply; they have personally cherished the political connection, and have inculcated fidelity to it with all their might. But their number is rapidly decreasing; as they die off natives take their places, and Canada will soon be in Canadian hands. Immigration generally is falling off; upper-class immigration is almost at an end, there being no longer a demand for anything but manual labour; and the influence of personal connection with England will cease to rule. The press is passing into the hands of natives, who are fast learning to hold their own against imported writing in literary skill, while they have an advantage in their knowledge of the country.

d. While the British troops remained in Canada, their officers formed a social aristocracy of the most powerful kind, and exercised a somewhat tyrannical influence over opinion. The traces of this influence still remain, but, with the exception of the reduced garrison of Halifax, the military occupation has ceased and is not likely to be renewed.

e. The Anglican Church in Canada clings to its position as a branch of the great state Church of England, and perhaps a faint hope of re-establishment may linger in the breasts of the bishops, who still retain the title of "lords." We have already said that the roots of Anglicanism in Canada do not appear to be strong, and its chief source of re-enforcement will be cut off by the discontinuance of upper-class emigration. It is rent in Canada, as in England, by the conflict between the Protestants and the Ritualists; and in Canada, there being no large endowments or legal system to clamp the hostile elements together, discord has already taken the form of disruption. As to the other churches, they have a connection with England, but not with England more than with the United States. The connection of Canadian Methodism with the United States is very close.

f. Orangeism is strong in British Canada, as indeed is every kind of association except the country. It retains its filial connection with its Irish parent, and is ultra-British on condition that Great Britain continues anti-papal. Old Irish quarrels are wonderfully tenacious of life, yet they must one day die, and Orangeism must follow them to the grave.

g. The social influence of English aristocracy, and of the little court of Ottawa over colonists of the wealthier class. With this, (to dismiss at once a theme more congenial to the social humorist than to the political observer) we may couple the influence of those crumbs of titular honour which English aristocracy sometimes allows to fall from its table into colonial mouths. If such forces cannot be said to be transient, the tendencies of human nature being perpetual, they may at least be said to be secondary; they do not affect the masses, and they do not affect the strong.

h. Antipathy to the Americans, bred by the old wars, and nursed by British influences, military and aristocratic, not without the assistance of the Americans themselves, who, in the case of the Fenian raids, and in other cases, have vented on Canada their feelings against England. This antipathy, so far as it prevails, leads those who entertain it to cling to an anti-American connection. But, generally speaking, it is very hollow. It does not hinder young Canadians from going by hundreds to seek their fortunes in the United States. It does not hinder wealthy Americans who have settled in Canada from finding seats at once in the Canadian Parliament. It never, in fact, goes beyond talk. So far as it partakes of the nature of contempt, it can hardly fail to be modified by the changed attitude of the British aristocracy, who have learned to exhibit something more than courtesy towards the victorious republic, while the Americans, it may be reasonably presumed, now that the cause of irritation is removed, will not think it wise to make enemies of a people whose destinies are inextricably blended with their own.

i. The special attachment naturally felt by the politicians, as a body, to the system with reference to which their parties have been formed, and with which the personal ambition of most of them is bound up. Perhaps, of all the forces which make for the present connection, this is the strongest; it has proved strong enough, when combined with the timidity and the want of independence which life-long slavery to a faction always breeds, to prevent any Canadian politician from playing a resolute part in such efforts as there have been to make Canada a nation. In some cases it is intensified by commercial connections with England, or by social aspirations, more or less definite, which have England for their goal. In this respect the interest of the politicians, as a class, is distinct from, and is liable to clash with, the real interest of the community at large. So, in the case of Scotland, it was the special interest of the politicians to resist the union, as, without special pressure and inducements, they would probably have persisted in doing. It was the interest of the people to accept the union, as the flood of prosperity which followed its acceptance clearly showed. In the case of Scotland, the interest of the people triumphed at last, and it will probably triumph at last in Canada.

Such, we say, are the chief forces that make for the existing connection; and we repeat that they appear to be secondary, and for the most part, transient. United, all these strands may make a strong cable; but, one by one they will give way, and the cable will cease to hold. This conviction is quite consistent with the admission that the connectionist sentiment is now dominant, especially in Ontario; that in Ontario it almost exclusively finds expression on the platform and in the press; and that the existence of any other opinions can only be inferred from reticence, or discovered by private intercourse. A visitor may thus be led to believe and to report that the attachment of the whole population to the present system is unalterable, and that the connection must endure forever. Those who have opportunities of looking beneath the surface may, at the same time, have grounds for thinking that, on economical subjects at least, the people have already entered on a train of thought which will lead them to a different goal.

What has been the uniform course of events down to the present time? Where are the American dependencies of Spain, Portugal, France, and Holland? Those on the continent, with unimportant exceptions, are gone, and those in the islands are going; for few suppose that Spain can keep Cuba very long. Of the English colonies on the continent, the mass, and those that have been long founded, have become independent;

and every one now sees, what clear-sighted men saw at the time, that the separation was inevitable, and must soon have been brought about by natural forces, apart from the accidental quarrel. If Canada has been retained it is by the reduction of imperial supremacy to a form. Self-government is independence; perfect self-government is perfect independence; and all the questions that arise between Ottawa and Downing Street, including the recent question about appeals, are successively settled in favour of self-government. Diplomatic union between two countries in different hemispheres, with totally different sets of external relations, common responsibility for each other's quarrels, and liability to be involved in each other's wars—these incidents of dependence remain, and these alone. Is it probable that this last leaf can continue to flutter on the bough forever? Lord Derby some years ago said that everybody knew that Canada must soon be an independent nation. Now he thinks that the tide of opinion has turned in favour of imperialism, and he turns with the tide. But what he takes for the turn of the tide may be merely the receding wave; and he forgets what the last wave swept away. It swept away the military occupation, with all its influences, political and social. Even since that time the commercial unity of the empire has been formally abandoned in the case of the Australian tariffs; and now the marriage-law of the colonies is clashing with that of the mother-country in the British House of Commons.

It is, perhaps, partly the recoil of feeling from a severance felt to be imminent, as well as the temporary influence of Conservative reaction in England, that has led to the revival in certain quarters, with almost convulsive vehemence, of the plan of imperial confederation. Certainly, if such a plan is ever to be carried into effect, this is the propitious hour. The spirit of aggrandizement is in the ascendant, and the colonies are all on good terms with the mother-country. Yet, of the statesmen who dally with the project, and smile upon its advocates, not one ventures to take a practical step toward its fulfilment. On the contrary, they are accessory to fresh inroads upon imperial unity, both in the judicial and in the fiscal sphere. Colonial governors talk with impressive vagueness of some possible birth of the imperial future, as though the course of events, which has been hurrying the world through a series of rapid changes for the last century, would now stand still, and impracticable aspirations would become practicable by the mere operation of time; but no colonial governor or imperial statesman has ventured to tell us, even in the most general way, to what it is that he looks forward, how it is to be brought about, or even what dependencies the confederation is to include. It is, therefore, needless to rehearse all the arguments against the feasibility of such a scheme. The difficulties which beset the union under the same parliamentary government of two countries in different parts of the world, with different foreign relations, and differing internally in political spirit, would, of course, be multiplied in the case of a union of twenty or thirty countries scattered over the whole globe, bound together by no real tie of common interest, and ignorant of each other's concerns. The first meeting of such a conclave would, we may be sure, develop forces of disunion far stronger than the vague sentiment of union arising from a very partial community of descent, and a very imperfect community of language, which would be the sole ground of the federation. Even to frame the agreement as to the terms of union with the shifting parties and ephemeral cabinets of a score of colonies under constitutional government would be no easy task. The two Parliaments, the one National, the other Federal, which it is proposed to establish in order to keep the national affairs of England separate from those of the Imperial Federation, would be liable to be brought into fatal conflict, and thrown into utter confusion by the ascendancy of different parties, say a war party and a peace party, in the National and Federal House. The veriest Chinese puzzle in politics would be a practicable constitution, if you could only get the real forces to conduct themselves according to the programme. It was not in the programme of Canadian confederation that the provinces should form separate interests in the Federal Parliament, and force the party leaders to bid against each other for their support; though any one who had studied actual tendencies in connection with the system of party government might have pretty confidently predicted that such would be the result. That England would allow questions of foreign policy, of armaments, and of peace and war, to be settled for her by any councils but her own, it is surely most chimerical to suppose. A swarm of other difficulties would probably arise out of the perpetual vicissitudes of the party struggle in each colony, the consequent inability of the delegates to answer for the real action of their own governments, and the estrangement of the delegates themselves from colonial interests and connections by their necessary residence in England. An essential condition of federation appears to be, tolerable equality among the members, or freedom from the ascendency of any overweening power; but, for a century to come, at least, the power of England in the Federal council would be overweering; and, to obviate this difficulty, some advocates of the scheme actually propose to repeal the union of England with Scotland and Ireland, so that she may be reduced to a manageable element of a Pan-Britannic confederation. They have surely little right to call other people disunionists, if any opprobrious meaning attaches to that term.

Supposing such a confederation to be practicable, of what use, apart from the vague feeling of aggrandizement, would it be? Where would be the advantage of taking from each of these young communities its political centre, which must also be, to some extent, its social and intellectual centre, and of accumulating them in the already overgrown capital of England? Does experience tell us that unlimited extension of territory is favourable to intensity of political life, or to anything which is a real element of happiness or of greatness? Does it not tell us that the reverse is the fact, and that the interest of history centres not in megalosaurian empires, but in states the body of which has not been out of proportion to the brain? Surely it would be well to have some distinct idea of the object to be attained before commencing this unparalleled struggle against geography and Nature. It can hardly be military strength. Military strength is not gained by dispersion of forces, by presenting vulnerable points in every quarter of the globe, or by embracing and undertaking to defend communities which, whatever may be their fighting qualities, in their policy are thoroughly unmilitary, and unmilitary will remain. Mr. Forster, in fact, gives us to understand that the Pan-Britannic Empire is to present a beneficent contrast to the military empires; that it is to be an empire of peace. But in that case it must, like other Quaker institutions, depend for its safety on the morality and forbearance of the holders of real and compact power, which is very far from being the dream of the advocates of "a great game."

In all these projects of Pan-Britannic Empire there lurks the assumption of a boundless multiplication of the Anglo-Saxon race. What are the grounds for this assumption? Hitherto it has appeared that races, as they grow richer, more luxurious, more fearful of poverty, more amenable to the restraints of social pride, have become less prolific. There is reason to suppose that in the United States the Anglo-Saxon race is far less prolific than the Irish, which is even supplanting the Anglo-Saxon in some districts of England, as the home-rule compliances of candidates for northern boroughs show. But the Irish element is small compared with the vast reservoir of industrial population in China, which is now beginning to overflow, and seems as likely as the Anglo-Saxon race to inherit Australia, where China has already a strong foothold, as well as the coast of the Pacific.

Canada, however, with regard to the problem of imperial confederation stands by herself, presenting, from her connection with the United States, difficulties from which in the case of the Australian colonies the problem is free. Of this some of the advocates of the policy of aggrandizement show themselves aware by frankly proposing to let Canada go.

It is taken for granted that political dependence is the natural state of all colonies, and that there is something unfilial and revolutionary in proposing that a colony should become a nation.

But what is a colony? We happen to have derived the term from a very peculiar set of institutions, those Roman colonies which had no life of their own but were merely the military and political outposts of the imperial republic. With the Roman colonies may be classed the Athenian *cleruchies* and, substituting the commercial for the political object, the factories of Carthage. But colonies, generally speaking, are migrations, and, as a rule, they have been independent from the beginning. Independent from the beginning, so far as we know, were the Phœnician colonies, Carthage herself among the number. Independent from the beginning were those Greek colonies in Italy which rapidly outran their mother cities in the race of material greatness. Independent from the beginning were the Saxon and Scandinavian colonies, and all those settlements of the Northern tribes which founded England herself with the other nations of modern Europe. So far as we can see, the original independence in each case was an essential condition of vigour and success. No Roman colony, Athenian *cleruchy*, or Carthaginian factory, ever attained real greatness. New England, the germ and organizer of the American communities, was practically independent for a long time after her foundation, the attention of the English Government being engrossed by troubles at home ; but she retained a slender thread of theoretic dependence by which she was afterward drawn back into a noxious and disastrous subordination. That thread was the feudal tie of personal allegiance, a tie utterly irrational when carried beyond the feudal pale, and by the recent naturalization treaties now formally abolished ; yet probably the main cause of the continued subjection of the transatlantic colonies, and of the calamities which flowed both to them and to the mother-country from that source.

It is natural that British statesmen should shrink from a formal act of separation, and that in their brief and precarious tenure of power they should be unwilling to take the burden and possible odium of such a measure upon themselves. But no one, we believe, ventures to say that the present system will be perpetual ; certainly not the advocates of imperial confederation, who warn us that, unless England by a total change of system draws her colonies nearer to her, they will soon drift farther away. Apart from lingering sentiment, it seems not easy to give reasons, so far as Canada is concerned, for struggling to prolong the present system.

THE POLITICAL DESTINY OF CANADA. 45

The motives for acquiring and holding dependencies in former days were substantial if they were not good. Spain drew tribute directly from her dependencies. England thought she drew it indirectly through her commercial system. It was also felt that the military resources of the colonies were at the command of the mother-country. When the commercial system was relinquished, and when self-government transferred to the colonies the control of their own resources, the financial and military motives ceased to exist. But the conservative imagination supplied their place with the notion of political tutelage, feigning—though, as we have seen, against all the evidence of history—that the colony, during the early stages of its existence, needed the political guidance of the mother-country in order to fit it to become a nation. Such was the language of colonial statesmen generally till the present conservative reaction again brought into fashion something like the old notion of aggrandizement, though for tribute and military contingents, the solid objects of the old policy, is now substituted "prestige." That the political connection between England and Canada is a source of military security to either, nobody, we apprehend, maintains. The only vulnerable point which England presents to the United States is the defenceless frontier of Canada; the only danger to which Canada is exposed is that of being involved in a quarrel between the aristocracy of England and the democracy of the United States. Defenceless, it is believed, the frontier of Upper Canada has been officially pronounced to be, and the chances of a desperate resistance to the invader in the French province can scarcely be rated very high. It is said that the British fleet would bombard New York. If Canada were in the hands of the enemy, the bombardment of New York would hardly alleviate her condition. But the bombardment of New York might not be an easy matter. The force of floating coast-defences seems now to be growing superior to that of ocean-going navies. Besides, America would choose the moment when England was at war with some other naval power. Soldiers and sailors, and of the best quality, England might no doubt find in Canada; but she would have to pay for them more than she pays for soldiers and sailors recruited at home. Whether morality is embodied in Bismarck or not, modern policy is; and Bismarck seems not to covet distant dependencies; he prefers solid and concentrated power.

"Commerce follows the flag," is a saying which

it seems can still be repeated by a statesman; but, like the notion that dependencies are a source of military strength, it is a mere survival from a departed system. Commerce followed the flag when the flag was that of a power which enforced exclusive trading. But exclusive trading has given way, as an imperial principle, to free-trade, and the colonies, in the exercise of their fiscal power of self-government, have dissolved the commercial unity of the empire. They frame their independent tariffs, laying, in some cases, heavy duties on English goods. It will hardly be contended that, apart from commercial legislation, colonial purchasers inquire whether goods were produced under the British flag. "The best customer," says Sir George Lewis, "which a nation can have, is a thriving and industrious community, whether it be dependent or independent. The trade between England and the United States is probably more profitable to the mother-country than it would have been if they had remained in a state of dependence upon her." As to Canada, what she needs, and needs most urgently, is free access to the market of her own continent, from which, as a dependency of England she is excluded by the customs line. With free access to the market of her own continent she might become a great manufacturing country, but manufactures are now highly specialized, and to produce with advantage you must produce on a large scale. Nor is the evil confined to manufactures; the farm-products of Canada are depreciated by exclusion from their natural market, and the lumber-trade, which is her great industry, will be in serious jeopardy, since, by the fall of wages in the States, the production of lumber there has been rendered nearly as cheap as it is in Canada, while Canadian lumber is subject to a heavy duty. The projects for opening markets in Australia merely serve to show how severely Canada feels the want of a market close at hand. Cut off any belt of territory commercially from the continent to which it belongs, industry will be stunted, the inflow of capital will be checked, and impoverishment will follow isolation. The Canadians will find this out in time, and the discovery will be the first step toward a change of system.

It is true that Canada has drawn a good deal of British capital into works little remunerative to the investors, though, perhaps, not more than the United States and other countries with which there was no political connection. But, if we consider credit as well as cash, the gain must be pronounced doubtful, and it is balanced by such a work as the Intercolonial Railway, into which Canada has been led by imperial influence, and which, after costing more than four millions sterling, will, as some leading Canadian men of business think, hardly "pay for the grease upon the wheels." The Pacific Railway, and the indemnity which Canada is forced to pay to British Columbia for the non-performance of an impracticable treaty, are too likely, in the opinion of many, to furnish another illustration of the expensiveness of the imperial connection.

That emigration is favourably influenced by political dependency is another lingering belief which seems now to have no foundation in fact, though it had in the days when emigration was a Government affair. The stream of emigration, in ordinary times, sets, as has often been proved, not toward Canada, but toward the United States; and of the emigrants who land in Canada a large proportion afterwards pass the line, while there is a constant exodus of French-Canadians from their own poor and overpeopled country (overpeopled so long as it is merely agricultural) to the thriving industries and the high wages of the States. Emigrants, whose object is to improve their material condition, are probably little influenced by political considerations; they go to the country which offers the best openings and the highest wages; but English peasants and artizans would be likely, if anything, to prefer the social elevation promised them in a land of equality to anything like a repetition of the social subjection in which they have lived at home, while by the Irishmen, escape from the British rule is deemed escape from oppression.

Whether the tutelage of the mother-country has ever been useful to a colony, even in its infancy, except where there was an actual need of military protection, is a question to which the language of the adherents of the colonial system themselves, when reviewing the history of colonial government, seems to suggest a negative reply. "Hitherto," says Mr. Roebuck, "those of our possessions termed colonies have not been governed according to any settled rule or plan. Caprice and chance have decided generally everything connected with them; and if success has in any case attended the attempts of the English people to establish colonies, that success has been obtained in spite of the mischievous intermeddling of the English Government, not in consequence of its wise and provident assistance." Such is the refrain of almost all the works on the colonies, whether they treat of the general administration or of some special question, such as that of the crown-lands, which appears to have been solved by Downing Street in various ways, but always wrong. Not by government, but by fugitives from the tyranny of government, the great American colony was founded; unaided and unregulated it grew, and laid the deep foundations of society in the New World. With tutelage came blundering, jobbery, mischief of all kinds, and at last a violent rupture, which injurious as it was to the mother-country, inflicted a still greater injury on the colony by launching it on the career of democracy with a violent revolutionary bias, whereas it needed a bias in favour of respect for authority. The presence of the British ambassador at the Centenary, was not only the ratification of the revolt, but the condemnation of the colonial system. After the American Revolution, the next step of the British Government was to divert the stream of English emigration from America—where there was an abundant room for it, and whither, the pioneer work having then been done, it would have been most profitably directed—to Australia, where the work had to be done over again, measures being at the same time taken to taint the new society with convict blood. To what good this scattering of English emigration has led, beyond the poetic conception of a boundless empire, it would seem difficult to say; and Canada, before she expresses conventional joy at the annexation of Fiji, should ask herself whether a new colony is anything more to her than a new competitor for the labour which is her prime need. In Canada herself, tutelage, while it was really exercised, led to every sort of evil. Government was jobbed by an oligarchy called the Family Compact, which Downing Street supported, not from bad motives, but from sheer ignorance of facts, till the misrule ended in the insurrection of 1837. Things have gone on smoothly only since real tutelage has departed, and left nothing but an image of royalty which reigns with gracious speeches and hospitality, but does not govern. There has been no want of good intentions on the part of English statesmen, nor would it be reasonable to suppose that there has been any special want of wisdom; probably no other statesmen would have done so well; but the task imposed on them was hopeless. One tree might as well be set to regulate the growth of another tree, as one nation to regulate the growth of another nation; and in this case the two trees are of different sorts and planted under different skies.

We can imagine the single mind of a **despot** moulding the political character of a colony, if not well, at least with adequate knowledge, with intelligence, and upon a definite plan. But England is not a single mind. England is the vast and motley mass of voters, including, since the Conservative Reform Bill, the most uneducated populace of the towns—people **who, in** politics, do not know their right hand from their left, who cannot tell the name of the leader of their own **party,** who vote for blue or yellow, and are led **by senseless** local cries, by bribery, or by beer. **These** are the political tutors of Canada, a country **in** which both wealth and education are more diffused than in England. How much does the average Englishman, or even the educated Englishman, know about Canadian politics? As much as Canadians know about the politics of Tasmania or the Cape. In "Phineas Finn," the **hero** of the tale, being under-secretary for the colonies, goes on a message to Marylebone "to find what the people there think about the Canadas." His report is: "Not one man in a thousand cares whether the Canadians prosper or fail to prosper. They care that Canada should not go to the States, because, though they don't love the Canadians, they do hate the Americans. That's about the feeling in Marylebone, and it's astonishing how like the Maryleboners are to the rest of the world." It will hardly be said that this is an unfair picture of a Londoner's normal frame of mind with regard to Canadian questions, or that Dorsetshire and Tipperary are better informed than London. When did a Canadian question influence an English election? How often is Canada mentioned in an election address? Canadian journals are never tired of exposing what they deem the scandalous ignorance of the leading journals of England on Canadian subjects, but they fail to draw the obvious moral. If the *Times* blunders, are the leaders of English opinion generally, and their constituents, likely to be better instructed and to decide aright? Burke, writing of the American Revolution, said that he could trace all the mischief "to the single source of not having had steadily before our eyes a general, comprehensive, and well-proportioned view of the whole of our dominions, and a just sense of their true bearings and relations." To say nothing of the ordinary holders of political power, in how many English statesmen, occupied as English statesmen are with home questions and party struggles, would Burke have found this comprehensive view, or the knowledge necessary for the formation of it? The colonial secretary himself is as often as not a man personally unacquainted with the colonies, not called to his post by special aptitude, but placed in it by party convenience. He must often depend for his information on such colonists as may find special access to Downing Street, or on the reports of governors, who, being images of royalty, are apt, like royalty, to be screened from truth. A peer he may be, but his peerage will not make him a providence. The annexation of Manitoba and of British Columbia to Canada—with which the latter, at all events, has no geographical conection—is by some thought to have been a disastrous, by all allowed to have been a most critical step: it was taken under the auspices of the late Lord Lytton, a brilliant and prolific novelist, brought into the government to make set speeches.

If any one supposes that the retention in Canada of the forms of monarchy excludes or mitigates any of the political evils, or even the coarseness to which democracy is liable in its crude condition, a year's residence in the country, a month's perusal of the party newspapers, or an hour's conversation with any Canadian man of business who has watched politics without taking part in them, will probably settle his opinion on that subject. That monarchical forms are no safeguard against corruption is a fact of which, unhappily, the colony has of late years had decisive proof. If the inquirer wishes to enlarge the basis of his induction, let him go through a file of Australian journals; he will there find a picture of public life, public character, and senatorial manners, decidedly below the level of the better States of the Union. Canada has escaped the elective judiciary, but so has Massachusetts; and both that and the removable civil service were the work not of real Republicans, but of the Democratic party—that is, of the slave-owning oligarchy of the South using as its instruments the Northern mob. Her exemption from the civil war and its fiscal consequences Canada owes merely to her separation from the States; it would have been the same had she been an independent nation. Had the political connection with Great Britain never existed, and had the weight of Canada been early thrown into the scale of freedom, there might have been no civil war.

In the case of the Pacific Railway scandal, the Governor-General may be said to have formally avowed himself a *fainéant*. He decided that he was absolutely bound to follow the advice of his ministers, even when those ministers lay under the heaviest charges of corruption, and even as to the mode in which the investigation into those charges should be conducted; and his conduct was approved by the home government. He has, therefore, no authority; and of nothing, nothing comes.

Most readers of the *Fortnightly* are probably prepared to regard with tolerance the proposition that figments and hypocrisies do no more good in politics than they do in general life. In Canadian politics they do much evil by blinding public men and the people generally to the real requirements of the situation. The hereditary principle was dead at its root; its work was done, and its age had passed away in the more advanced portion of humanity when the communities of the New World were founded. It lingers on, as things do linger on, in its native soil; but it can furnish no sound basis for government in the soil of reason and equality. The only conceivable basis for government in the New World is the national will; and the political problem of the New World is how to build a strong, stable, enlightened, and impartial government on that foundation. That it is a very difficult problem, daily experience in Canada, as well as in the neighbouring republic, shows, and to be successfully solved it must be seen in its true bearings, which the ostensible retention of the hereditary principle as the security for good and stable government obscures. Canada, though adorned with the paraphernalia of eight constitutional monarchies (one central and seven provincial), is a democracy of the most pronounced kind; the Governor-General was not wrong in saying that she is more democratic than the United States, where the President is an elective king, and where the Senate, which, though elective, is conservative, possesses great power, whereas the nominated Senate of Canada is a cipher. Demagogism and the other pests of democratic institutions are not to be conjured away by forms and phrases; they can be repressed and prevented from ruining the state only by developing remedial forces of a really effective kind, and by adjusting the actual machinery of the constitution so as to meet the dangers which experience may reveal. The treason-law of the Plantagenets with which, as well as with the Lord Chamberlain's code of precedence, Canada is endowed, is not of much use to her while she is left without any legal means of repressing her real cancer, political corruption. Loyalty to the *fainéant* deputy of a distant crown may be in a certain sense real; it may be felt by those who profess it; but it probably does not often prompt to a good political action, and it certainly never restrains from a bad one. Among Canadians, as among American politicians, the most "truly loyal" are often the most unscrupulous and corrupt. They are often, through the whole course of their public lives, disloyal to everything that represents public honour and the public good. A provincial court adds flunkyism to demagogism without making the demagogue less profligate, less dangerous, or less vile. It does not even make him less coarse. No refining influence can really be exercised by a few dinners and receptions even over the small circle which attends them; while the social expenditure and display which are imposed on the Governor-General as the condition of his popularity in the colony, and of the maintenance of his reputation at home, are anything but a wholesome example for colonial society, which, on the contrary, needs an example of hospitality and social enjoyment cultivated in an easy and inexpensive way.

At present the bane of Canada is party government without any question on which parties can be rationally or morally based. The last question of sufficient importance to form a rational and moral basis for a party was that of the Clergy Reserves and the Church Establishment, since the settlement of which there has been absolutely no dividing line between the parties or assignable ground for their existence, and they have become mere factions, striving to engross the prizes of office by the means which faction everywhere employs. The consequences are, the increasing ascendancy of the worst men, and the political demoralization of a community, which, if a fair chance were given it, would furnish as sound a basis for good government as any community in the world. Of course, England cannot be charged with introducing the party system into Canada; but she does fling over it the glamour of British association, and beguile a country really abandoned to all the instability and all the degrading influences of government by faction with the ostensible stability and dignity of the hereditary crown. Indeed, the provision in the draft of confederation that both the parties should be considered in the first nomination of senators is, perhaps, the only authoritative recognition which the party system has ever received. In common with the other colonies,

THE POLITICAL DESTINY OF CANADA.

Canada is deemed happy in being endowed with a counterpart of the British Constitution. The British Constitution putting aside the legal forms and phrases, is government by party; and whatever government by party may be in England, where there are some party questions left, in Canada it is a most noxious absurdity, and is ruining the political character of the people.

When Canadian Nationalists say that patriotism is a good thing, they are told to keep their wisdom for the copy-books; and the rebuke would be just if those who administer it would recognise the equally obvious truth that there can be no patriotism without nationality. In a dependency there is no love of the country, no pride in the country; if an appeal is made to the name of the country, no heart responds as the heart of an Englishman responds when an appeal is made in the name of England. In a dependency every bond is stronger than that of country, every interest prevails over that of the country. The province, the sect, Orangeism, Fenianism, Freemasonry, Oddfellowship, are more to the ordinary Canadian than Canada. So it must be while the only antidote to sectionalism in a population with strongly-marked differences of race and creed is the sentiment of allegiance to a distant throne. The young Canadian leaving his native country to seek his fortune in the States feels no greater wrench than a young Englishman would feel in leaving his county to seek his fortune in London. Want of nationality is attended, too, with a certain want of self-respect, not only political but social, as writers on colonial society and character have observed. Wealthy men in a dependency are inclined to look to the Imperial country as the social centre and the mark of their social ambition, if not as their ultimate abode, and not only their patriotic munificence but their political and social services are withdrawn from the country of their birth.

Mr. Trollope finds himself compelled to confess that in passing from the United States into Canada you pass "from a richer country into one that is poorer, from a greater country into one that is less." You pass from a country embracing in itself the resources of a continent, into one which is a narrow section of that continent cut off commercially from the rest; you pass from a country which is a nation into a country which is not a nation.

On the other hand, there were reasons which, not only to patriotic Canadians, but to patriotic Americans who took a comprehensive view of the interests of their country, seemed strong, for wishing that Canada should remain politically separate from the United States. Democracy is a great experiment, which might be more safely carried on by two nations than by one. By emulation, mutual warning and correction, mutual supplementation of defects, they might have helped each other in the race, and steadied each other's steps; a balance of opinion might have been established on the continent, though a balance of power cannot; and the wave of dominant sentiment which spreads over that vast democracy like the tide running in over a flat, might have been usefully restricted in its sweep by the dividing line. Nor was there any insurmountable obstacle in the way. Canada is wanting in unity of race; but not more so than Switzerland, whose three races have been thoroughly welded together by the force of nationality. She is wanting in compactness of territory, but not more so, perhaps than some other nations— Prussia, for instance—have been. In this latter respect, however the situation has been seriously altered by the annexation of Manitoba and British Columbia, which in their present raw condition have no influence beyond that of distant possessions, but which, when peopled and awakened to commercial life, will be almost irresistibly attracted by the economical forces to the States which adjoin them on the south, and will thus endanger the cohesion of the whole confederacy. The very form of the Dominion indeed, drawn out and attenuated as it is by these unnatural additions, apart from the attractive influence of Minnesota and California, would seriously imperil its political unity, as will be seen, if, instead of taking Canada as it is presented by the political map, the boundary-line is drawn between the habitable portion and that which belongs only to arctic frosts. In the debate on confederation it was urged by the advocates of the measure that seven sticks, though separately weak, when bound together in a fagot would be strong. "Yes," was the reply, but not so seven fishing rods tied together by the ends."

As to the expense of a national government, it would probably not be greater than that of the governor-generalship and the seven lieutenant-governorships is at present. Diplomacy in these days of rapid communication may be cheaply done, and Canada would not need much of it: she has no Eastern question.

The queston of military security has reference solely to the danger to be apprehended on the side of the **United States**; and **danger on** the side of the **United States,** supposing Canada disentangled from **English** quarrels, we believe **that** there is none. The Americans, as has **been repeatedly** observed, have since the fall of slavery given every proof of an unambitious disposition. They disbanded their vast **armaments** immediately on the close of the civil war, **without waiting** even for the Alabama question to be settled; they have refused to **annex** St. Domingo; they have observed a policy of strict non-intervention in the case of Cuba, which they might have made **their own** with the greatest ease; they have declined **to take ad**vantage **of** the pretexts furnished them **in abundance, by** border outrages, of conquering Mexico; it is very doubtful whether they would even have purchased **Alaska, if** Mr. Seward had not drawn them by secret negotiations into a position from which they could **not well** retreat. Slavery wanted conquest for the creation of new slave States, but **with** slavery the spirit of aggression appears **to have** died. Welcome Canada into the Union **if** she came of her own accord, the Americans no doubt would. They would be strangely wanting **in** wisdom if they did **not; for she** would bring them as **her** dower not only complete immunity **from** attack, and great

E

economical advantages, but a political accession of the most valuable kind in the shape of a population, not like that of St. Domingo, Cuba or Mexico, but trained to self-government, and capable of lending fresh strength and vitality to republican institutions. It is true that slavery having been abolished, the urgent need of adding to the number of the free States in order to counterbalance the extension of slavery in the councils of the Union no longer exists; but there are still in the population of the United States large elements essentially non-republican—the Irish, the emigrants from Southern Germany, the negroes—to which, perhaps, may be added a considerable portion of Southern society itself, which can hardly fail to retain something of its old character while it continues to be composed of a superior and an inferior race. Against these non-republican elements, the really republican element still needs to be fortified by all the reinforcements which it can obtain. Welcome Canada, therefore, into the Union the Americans no doubt would. But that they have the slightest inclination to lay violent hands upon her, that such a thought ever enters their minds, no one who has lived among them, and heard the daily utterances of a by no means reticent people, can believe. Apart from moral principle, they know that, though a despotic Government may simply annex, a republic must incorporate, and that to incorporate four millions of unwilling citizens would be to introduce into the republic a most dangerous mass of disaffection and disunion. That the Americans have been litigious in their dealings with Canada is true; but litigiousness is not piracy; and, as we have already said, the real object of their irritation has not been Canada, but England. The Monroe doctrine was held by Canning as well as by Monroe; and, irrespectively of any desire of aggrandizement, the intrusion of an American power in Europe would give as much umbrage to England as the intrusion of the English power in their own continent gives to the people of the United States. That the Americans would feel pride in behaving generously towards a weaker state, will appear credible only to those who have seen enough of them to know that, though supposed to care for nothing but the dollar, they have in reality a good deal of pride.

As an independent nation, Canada would, of course, be at liberty to negotiate freely for the removal of the customs-line between herself and the United States, and for admission to all the commercial **advantages of her own** continent. At **present not only is she trammelled by** imperial considerations, **but it can hardly** be expected that the American **Government** will place itself on **a lower** international level than that of England by **treating** with a dependency as a nation, especially **as there** are constant intimations that **the dependency is** retained **and is** being nursed **up** with **the** view of making it a rival **power to the United** States, and thus introducing into the **continent the germs of future** jealousy, and **possibly of war.**

That **Canada can ever** be made a rival power to the United States—that, if **she is** only kept **long** enough in a state **of dependence,** there will **be an** indefinite increase of **her** population and her strength—seems to be little better than rhetorical fancy. The **barrier of** slavery being removed, the **set** of **population** is likely to be, not toward the frozen **north,** where the winter, besides suspending **labour** and business, eats up the **produce of the summer** in the **cost of** fuel, but **toward those countries in which warmth** is provided **by the sun, and** work **may** be carried on during **the whole year. The notion** that the north **is the natural seat of** empire seems to have no **more solid foundation.** It is apparently a loose generalization from the success of the northern tribes which conquered the Roman Empire. It is forgotten that those northern warriors had not only been hardened by exposure to the full severity of the northern climate, but picked by the most rigorous process of natural selection. Stove-heat is not less enervating than the heat of the sun. But a nation Canada, so far as we can see, might have been, had the attempt been vigorously made at the propitious moment, when owing to the effects of the civil war in the United States, the balance of prosperity was decidedly in her favour, when her financial condition appeared immensely superior to that of her neighbour, and when the spirit of her people had been stirred by confederation. That opportunity was allowed to pass, and, in all probability, it will never return.

A movement in favour of nationality there was —one which had a twofold claim to sympathy, because it was also a movement against faction and corruption, and which, though it has failed, has left honourable traces on public life. But it was not strong enough to make head against the influences which have their centre in the little court of Ottawa, and the attacks of the lower class of politicians, who assailed it with the utmost ferocity, seeing clearly that the success of the higher impulse would not suit their game. Moreover, the French province interposed between the British provinces of the east and west, is a complete non-conductor, and prevents any pulsation from running through the whole body. It must further be owned that, in industrial communities, the economical motives are stronger than the political, and that the movement in favour of Canadian nationality had only political motives on its side. Perhaps the appearance of a great man might after all have turned the scale; but dependencies seldom produce great men.

Had the movement in favour of nationality succeeded, the first step would have been a legislative union, which would in time have quelled sectionalism, and made up for the deficiency of material size and force by moral solidity and unity of spirit. Canada, as was said before, is hardly a proper subject for federal government, which requires a more numerous group of states and greater equality between them. Confederation as it exists, we repeat, has done little more than develop the bad side of democratic government. A project is now on foot for a legislative union between Nova Scotia, New Brunswick, and Prince Edward Island; but this will only make matters worse by reducing the number of important states to three (Manitoba and British Columbia being in the merest infancy), two of which will be always combining against the third. That there would have been opposition to a legislative union of the whole of Canada on the part of Quebec is more than probable; but Quebec, if she had been handled with determination would most likely have given way.

Canadian nationality being a lost cause, the ultimate union of Canada with the United States appears now to be morally certain; so that nothing is left for Canadian patriotism but to provide that it shall be a union indeed, and not an annexation; an equal and honourable alliance like that of Scotland and England, not a submission of the weaker to the stronger; and at the same time that the political change shall involve no change of any other kind in the relations of Canada with her mother-country. The filaments of union are spreading daily, though they may be more visible to the eye of one who sees Canada at intervals than to that of a constant resident. Intercourse is being increased by the extension of railways; the ownership and management of the railways themselves are forming an American interest in Canada; New York is becoming the pleasure, and, to some extent, even the business, capital of Canadians; American watering-places are becoming their summer resort; the periodical literature of the States, which is conducted with extraordinary spirit and ability, is extending its circulation on the northern side of the line; and the Canadians who settle in the States are multiplying the links of family connection between the two countries. To specify the time at which a political event will take place is hardly ever possible, however assured the event itself may be; and in the present instance the occurrence depends not only on the circumstances of Canada, where, as we have seen, there is a great complication of secondary forces, but on the circumstances of the United States. If the commercial depression which at present prevails in Canada continues or recurs; if Canadian manufacturers are seen to be dying under the action of the customs-line; if owing to the depression or to over-costly undertakings, such as the Pacific Railway, financial difficulties arise; if, meantime the balance of prosperity, which is now turning, shall have turned decisively in favour of the United States, and the reduction of their debt shall have continued at the present rate—the critical moment may arrive, and the politicians, recognizing the voice of Destiny, may pass in a body to the side of continental union. It will be fortunate if a misunderstanding between the Canadian Government and Downing Street, about some question such as that respecting the pecuniary claims of British Columbia, which is now assuming such exaggerated proportions, does not supervene to make the final dissolution of the political tie a quarrel instead of an amicable separation.

To Canada the economical advantages of continental union will be immense; to the United States its general advantages will not be less so. To England it will be no menace, but the reverse; it will be the introduction into the Councils of the United States, on all questions, commercial as well as diplomatic, of an element friendly to England, the influence of which will be worth far more to her than the faint and invidious chance of building up Canada as a rival to the United States. In case of war, her greatest danger will be removed. She will lose neither wealth nor strength; probably she will gain a good deal of both. As to glory, we cannot do better than quote in conclusion the words of Palmerston's favourite colleague, and the man to whom he, as was generally supposed, wished to bequeath his power:

"There are supposed advantages flowing from the possession of dependencies, which are expressed in terms so general and vague that they cannot be referred to any determinate head. Such, for example, is the glory which a country is supposed to derive from an extensive colonial empire. We will merely remark, upon this imagined advantage, that a nation derives no true glory from any possession which produces no assignable advantage to itself or to other communities. If a country possesses a dependency from which it derives no public revenue, no military or naval strength, and no commercial advantages or facilities for emigration, which it would not equally enjoy though the dependency were independent, and if, moreover, the dependency suffers the evils which (as we shall show hereafter) are the almost inevitable consequences of its political condition, such a possession cannot justly be called glorious."

REPLY.

THE POLITICAL DESTINY OF CANADA.*

BY SIR FRANCIS HINCKS.

It happened quite accidentally that the *Fortnightly Review* of 1st April, containing an essay on "The Political Destiny of Canada," was placed in my hands for perusal on the 23rd of that month (St. George's Day), soon after I had read a report of a sermon preached on the preceding afternoon to the St. George's Society of Montreal by its Chaplain, the Rev. R. W. Norman. I was of course, much struck with the widely different views of the authors of the essay and the sermon, both of whom are Englishmen, both graduates of the University of Oxford, and both residents in Canada during a comparatively short

---

* This article was sent by me to a friend in England for insertion either in the *Fortnightly Review*, or in some other periodical of standing.—F. H.

period. It at once occurred to me, that it might be interesting to the readers of the *Fortnightly* to be put in possession of the views of those who share Mr. Norman's sentiments, and I further thought that I might, without presumption, become their exponent. I, like the two gentlemen whom I have named, am a native of the United Kingdom, but I adopted Canada as my home forty-five years ago. It is more than forty years since I began to take an active part in public life; it has been my lot to have been connected with both of the political parties, those styled Conservatives and Reformers, but I am now, and have been for the last three years, unconnected with party, having altogether withdrawn from politics. I think that, under the foregoing circumstances, I may claim to be as well acquainted with the sentiments of the people of Canada as the author of the essay in the *Fortnightly*, for whom I entertain all the respect to which his great abilities entitle him. I presume that I may treat the essayist as a Canadian, in the same sense as I look on all natives of the United Kingdom who adopt Canada as their country. The essayist has specially devoted himself to foster Canadian nationality, but I must own that, although I have read a great deal that he has written for the Canadian press for some years, his essay in the *Fortnightly* surpasses anything I have seen from his pen in hostility to British connexion, and in abuse of Canadian politicians of all shades of party. I am bound to admit that the essayist is indiscriminate in his censure, and that he would be able to prove his case against either of the political parties from what they habitually say of each other; while, on the other hand, each would protest against the truth of the charges as applicable to his own party. It seems to me rather inconsistent that one who admits that he has laboured unsuccessfully in Canada to create a Canadian nationality and to destroy the political parties which he found in existence on his arrival in the country, should endeavour to influence English public opinion on a subject in which Canada is chiefly interested, and which the essayist admits, ought to be considered with reference to the interests of Canada.

As, however, the essayist has selected his arena, it seems but fair that those who entirely dissent from his views should have a fair hearing. I may call attention to the language employed by the essayist in referring to Canadian politicians. The "truly loyal," he says, "are often the most unscrupulous and corrupt," they are often "disloyal to everything that represents public honour and the public good." The parties have become "mere factions;" the consequences are the increasing ascendency of the worst men, and the political demoralization of a community." The movement in favour of nationality was "against faction and corruption," but was not strong enough "to make head against the influences which have their centre in the little court at Ottawa, and the attacks of the lower class of politicians, who assailed it with the utmost ferocity." I need not multiply extracts condemnatory of Canadian politicians of both parties, but I think that I am not unwarranted in assuming that the bitterness which pervades the essay must have been intensified by the feeling that the writer had completely failed in his attempt to create a public opinion in Canada favourable to his peculiar views. The attacks to which I have referred have chiefly influenced me in referring to the sermon preached by the Rev. Mr. Norman. That gentleman is in no sense a party politician, and yet living, as he does, in the principal city of Canada, and in daily intercourse with gentlemen of intelligence and property, he is as free from those influences so much deprecated by the essayist, as any one can be. I propose to submit a few extracts from Mr. Norman's sermon as an introduction to the criticism which I shall venture to offer on Mr. Goldwin Smith's paper.

"We all know what power a simple strain possesses to recall, with vivid and startling force, places, persons, conversations. The music of our own National Anthem has that magic power. It makes the heart beat, the blood to flow, the pulse to throb. May it never lose that magnetic tenacity upon the hearts of British subjects, especially those who are British born. But the text, though it supplies us with the note of patriotism, while its tender charm must touch every heart, is, in one important respect, haply inapplicable to us. This is not a strange land. We are not here as captives taunted by cynical oppressors. Though in another hemisphere, we see our tokens, and feel that we are among friends.

. . . . . .

"It is the love to the dear Mother Country, and through her, the love of her children, that is the source of this Society's existence. That is the bond which unites us all one to the other. It is the strong affection we bear our Queen and Country, the admiration we all entertain for her institutions, that make us recognize and desire to help as brethren those who claim old England as the conntry of their birth.

. . . .

"The St. George's Society reminds us that we share the greatness, the glory, the freedom of that land upon whose sacred soil the exile can tread in safety; the land which offers an asylum to the unfortunate, the unhappy, no matter who they be; the land that brooks not slavery, and whereon for centuries no foreign invader has been able to plant his foot. This Dominion is great in itself; greater still in its future prospects. But its greatness is enhanced by its connection with the Mother Land, and it shares, through common origin, in the illustrious past of the great British nation. Surely of this country it may to a certain extent be said that the honours on the crest of England are garlands for the head of Canada. It is no proof of national vigour to ignore the past, and live only in the present. While, therefore, we love Canada; while we are ready to serve her interests and promote her advancement, let us still turn a loving glance across the broad sea to the mother of us all. Happily, loyalty is a master principle in the heart of a Canadian. Like justice, of which the Roman poet wrote, which quitting the world, yet lingered in rural abodes and pastoral pursuits; so loyalty, even if about to quit this earth, which I trust is not to be, yet tarries here, and there is no fear of its extinction. And the loyalty of Canadians is of the true, old-fashioned type—unselfish, faithful; the loyalty of the free."

Although Mr. Norman addressed the language that I have quoted, especially to Englishmen, I believe that it contains a faithful exposition of the sentiments entertained by the Canadian people of all nationalities towards the mother-country. I believe, moreover, that there has been no period in the history of Canada when its inhabitants were so loyal, as at the very time when the writer in the *Fortnightly* has considered it his duty "to cast its political horoscope," and to assure the people of England that its destination is absorption in the adjoining Republic. When I first entered public life I am firmly convinced that the majority of Canadians were thoroughly alienated in their feelings, from the British Crown. Those who engaged in the rebellion of 1837 constituted but a fraction of those who were discontented with the old colonial system of government, to which Lord Durham's report gave a death-blow. The revolution, as the establishment of parliamentary government may properly be termed, was followed by feelings of intense bitterness on the part of the old Tory, or, as they styled themselves, the loyalist party. Great allowance must be made for their feelings under the circumstances. A portion of the popular party had engaged in rebellion, and the Tory party had aided in its suppression. When parliamentary government was established, the Reformers obtained political power, and the exasperation of the loyalists was manifested by the burning of the Parliament House, by insults to Governor-General the Earl of Elgin, and, finally, by the annexation manifesto, which, though repudiated by the political chiefs, was

F

signed chiefly by persons belonging to the Tory party. This was in 1849. In 1854 there was a complete disruption of parties. During the 13 years which had elapsed from the union of the Canadas, the old Reform party of Ontario had been in strict alliance with the French Canadians, but in 1854 a disagreement among members of the Reform party, which had existed two or three years, culminated in a complete split, and the result was the formation of a Government party consisting of the old Conservatives, the French Canadians, and those Reformers from Ontario who adhered to the old Government, the Opposition being those Ontario Reformers who had been dissatisfied with the Reform Government, and a French Canadian Liberal party, which included many English, although the Lower Canada British party adhered to the new Government. The practical effect of these changes was to allay to a great extent the old animosities between the British and the French. Since that period there has been no serious agitation for political change, and although I regret to have to acknowledge that there is deplorable party bitterness at present, yet the leaders of both political parties are unquestionably sincerely loyal, and friendly to the subsisting connection with Great Britain. It must surely strike with amazement English readers of the essay in the *Fortnightly*, that in a House of Commons consisting of upwards of 200 members, not one member has ventured, either in the House or at the hustings, to propose the severance of the subsisting connexion with Great Britain.

Widely as I differ from the views of the writer in the *Fortnightly* as to the " Political Destiny of Canada," there are portions of his essay in which he has given expression to Canadian opinion, on points on which it is highly desirable that our fellow-countrymen in England should be correctly informed. The principal of these is Canadian nationality, of which the essayist was, as he admits, once an advocate, and for which he still evinces a desire. He admits, however, that it is "a lost cause," and as he is determined not to believe in the continuation of the present connexion, he is bound to maintain that union with the United States is "morally certain." I am not presumptuous enough to declare that the subsisting connexion must be perpetual, but I am decidedly of opinion, in common, as I have reason to know, with the leaders of both political parties, that if at any future period, owing to causes which it is impossible to foresee at present, a disruption of our connexion with Great Britain were to become necessary, there would inevitably be union with the United States and not an Independent Republic. It is desirable that those English politicians who sometimes look with complacency on the severance of the connexion, should, be aware that its result would be very different from what they imagine. I likewise concur with the essayist that all the projects of Pan-Britannic Empire are visionary in the greatest degree. I refer to the subject merely because the essayist has done so, and because some scheme of the kind has found favour in England, though as justly observed—" of the statesmen who dally with the project and smile upon its advocates, not one ventures to take a practical step towards its fulfilment." No such scheme has ever found favour in Canada.

Having noticed the points on which I concur with the writer in the *Fortnightly*, I shall proceed to state those on which I entirely differ with him. It may be convenient to state my objections under the following heads : 1st. Errors in matters of fact; 2nd. Inconsistencies; 3rd. Erroneous reasoning. Under the first head the most important errors are those which attach undeserved blame to the Imperial

Government. Reference is made to the "Intercolonial Railway, into which Canada has been led by Imperial influence, and which after, costing more than four millions sterling, will, as some leading Canadian men of business think, hardly pay for the grease upon the wheels." A more unjust charge never was made. It has certainly not been the practice of the Imperial Government either to suggest the construction of public works in Canada, or to interfere with them in any way. The scheme for the construction of an Intercolonial Railway originated in Nova Scotia, and it was on the joint application of the separate Provinces that the Imperial Government authorized Royal Engineer officers to conduct a survey. The principal of these, Major Robinson, located a line, after which the three Provinces conferred as to the construction and as to the proportions of expense to be incurred by each. New Brunswick positively refused co-operation unless a different line from that recommended was adopted, and the other Provinces—Nova Scotia most reluctantly, Canada willingly—concurred with New Brunswick. Thereupon the Imperial Government, in 1852, stated that the Imperial guarantee asked as a favour, could only be given to the line recommended by Major Robinson. The negotiations were thereupon broken off. When the delegates, several years afterwards, met to consider confederation, the construction of the Intercolonial Railway was made one of the conditions of the union, and again the Imperial guarantee was sought. To what extent Imperial influence may have been used in favour of the original line I am hardly in a position to state, not having been in the country at the time; but what I do know is, first, that a majority of Canadian ministers were in favour of the line adopted, and secondly, that the utmost extent of interference on the part of the Imperial Government was to make the adoption of the line favoured by them a condition of their guarantee which every reasonable person will admit they had a perfect right to do. I submit that the charge in the essay is not justified by the facts which I have stated.

The next imputation against the Imperial Government which I shall notice, is the allegation that the annexion of British Columbia "was taken under the auspices of the late Lord Lytton, a brilliant and prolific novelist, brought into the Government to make set speeches." I may consider with this another allegation :—"The Pacific Railway, and the indemnity which Canada is forced to pay to British Columbia for the non-performance of an impracticable treaty, are too likely in the opinion of many, to furnish another illustration of the expensiveness of the Imperial connexion. The sole foundation for these charges is the fact that Lord Lytton, when Secretary of State, prior to the year 1859, expressed some opinions as to the different modes of governing Vancouver's Island and British Columbia. I have not thought it worth while to ascertain precisely what occurred at that time, simply because Lord Lytton had no more responsibility for the admission of British Columbia into the Canadian Confederation, than the writer of the essay himself. Delegates were sent from British Columbia to Canada, and the terms of confederation were arranged at conferences between the Canadian Ministers and those Delegates, and were subsequently ratified by the Canadian Parliament. The construction of the Pacific Railway was provided for by the terms of union, and has been a *bete noir* of the essayist, as well as of the political party opposed to the government which undertook it. It has been a subject of unceasing reproach by each political party against its antagonist; but no party politician in Canada has ever ventured to throw blame on the Imperial Government as the essayist has done. In connection with

British Columbia, the annexation of Manitoba "is by some thought to have been a disastrous, by all allowed to have been a most critical step." The Imperial Government did not in any way promote the annexation of Manitoba, which was sought for during many years by Canadian emigrants to the North-west, and by their countrymen; but when negotiations for the acquisition of the territory were set on foot, it lent its good offices to the contracting parties, Canada and the Hudson Bay Company.

I have specified what I consider grave errors in matters of fact. The transparent object of the writer was to convince his English readers that, owing to the errors of Secretaries of State, who are said to be often "personally unacquainted with the Colonies—not called to their post by special aptitude, but placed in it by party convenience," Canada had suffered grievous injuries; and yet I affirm, without fear of contradiction from the leaders of the opposing parties in Canada, that, during the ten years that have elapsed since Confederation, there has not been the slightest complaint of improper interference on the part of the Imperial Government with the Government of Canada. During that period there has been a Liberal Government in England, with a Conservative Government in Canada, and now there is a Conservative Government in England and a Liberal one in Canada, but so good an understanding exists that no one is ever apprehensive of difficulty. I proceed to consider—

2ndly. The inconsistencies of the essayist. In order to establish his case he was bound to prove that dependencies could not be satisfactorily governed. "The very name 'colony' is obnoxious, derived from a very peculiar set of institutions, those Roman Colonies which had no life of their own, but were merely the military and political outposts of the Imperial Republic." All the successful colonies were those "independent from the beginning. Even New England, the germ and organizer of the American communities, was practically independent for a long time after her foundation." The writer proceeds to descant on the sufferings endured by dependencies, citing from an old speech pamphlet of Mr. Roebuck's that "our colonies have not been governed according to any settled rule or plan," that "caprice and chance have decided generally everything connected with them," and that if there has been success it has been obtained "in spite of the mischievous intermeddling of the English Government, not in consequence of its wise and provident assistance." This, it is said, is "the refrain of almost all the works on the Colonies." England cannot have colonies or dependencies because England is the vast and motley mass of voters including, since "the Conservative Reform Bill, the most uneducated populace of the towns, people who in politics do not know their right hand from their left." Even "Phineas Finn" is cited as an authority to prove how little England is competent to maintain a Colonial system. Phineas reports of the people of Marylebone, "not one man in a thousand cares whether the Canadians prosper or fail to prosper, They care that Canada should not go to the States, because though they don't love the Canadians they do hate the Americans." This, the essayist asserts, is not "an unfair picture of a Londoner's normal frame of mind." And very similar is that of the inhabitants of Dorsetshire and Tipperary. I grant it all, just as I grant that a Canadian Londoner, in his home on the banks of the Canadian Thames, cares not whether the inhabitants of Marylebone prosper or fail to prosper. The Canadians have just as much influence over English questions, as the English over theirs; and when it is triumphantly asked, "When did a Canadian question influence an English election." I simply reply, "When did an English question influence a Canadian election." But I have dwelt, I trust, sufficiently on the essayist's argument against the Colonial connexion, founded on the incompetency of English electors to govern remote dependencies. I purpose now to show, from another part of the same essay, that the argument has not the slightest application. Referring to the "course of events" in regard to the colonies of Spain, Portugal, France, and Holland, the essayist proceeds: "If Canada has been retained, it is by the reduction of Imperial supremacy to a form. Self-government is independence—perfect self-government is perfect independence; and all the questions that arise between Ottawa and Downing Street, including the recent questions about appeals, are successively settled in favour of self-government." What then becomes of the argument based on the "uneducated populace" of the English towns, and on the opinion of Phineas Finn's Maryleboner? The truth is, that "the refrain of almost all the works on the Colonies" had reference to that old system when, to use the language of the essayist, "Government was jobbed by an oligarchy; whereas the statement that "self-government is independence, and that all the questions that arise between Ottawa and Downing Street are successively settled in favour of self-government," is a faithful description of the present Canadian system.

In his bitter censure of Parliamentary Government the essayist has fallen into a glaring inconsistency. The Government is said to be the bane of Canada, because "there is no question on which parties can be rationally or morally based," consequently the parties have become "mere factions, striving to engross the prizes of office." Such allegations abound through the essay, but, on the other hand, there are some admissions which would indicate to any experienced politician that there are important questions on which parties may properly be divided.

I could enumerate several, but as my present object is merely to establish my charge of inconsistency, I shall content myself by referring to two questions noticed in the essay. Surely the question of Protection is one on which political parties might properly join issue. The essayist states that "Canada at this moment is the scene of a protectionist movement, led curiously enough by those 'Conservative politicians' who are loudest in their professions of loyalty to Great Britain." The divisions in the Canadian House of Commons were, with two or three exceptions, strictly party, and the English newspapers have expressed their satisfaction with the result. It does not strike me as at all curious that Conservative politicians should have a predilection for protection, but on the other hand it does appear to me rather extraordinary that so advanced a liberal as the essayist should be an extreme protectionist. I am persuaded that the members of the Conservative opposition are not of opinion that their views on this question are inconsistent with their loyalty to the crown, but I only refer to them here to prove that there is an important question on which political parties are divided. There is yet another, viz., British Columbia and the Pacific Railway. On these questions Canadian parties are in avowed antagonism. The essayist admits fully their importance, for he thinks that it will be fortunate if some question " such as that respecting the pecuniary claims of British Columbia, which is now assuming such exaggerated proportions, does not supervene to make the final dissolution of the political tie a quarrel instead of an amicable separation." Surely a question from which such serious consequences are apprehended, is one important enough for the consideration of political parties in Canada, by whom alone it must be solved. I need hardly observe that there is not the slightest danger of any misunderstanding between the Imperial and Canadian Governments on any such question, nor so far as I can foresee, on any other; and if the essayist really believes what he has stated, that "all questions are successively settled in favour of self-government," he need be under no apprehension on the subject. I think it must be admitted that I have proved by his own language that the essayist is most inconsistent in alleging that there are no questions in Canada on which parties can be honestly formed. Another inconsistency will be found in those passages of the essay in which the author treats of the Roman Catholic element in our population. There is, indeed, not only inconsistency; there is error in a matter of fact. It is assumed that the French Canadian and Irish Catholics, constituting 1,400,000 of the population, are anything but friends to British connection. These it is said, must be deducted in order to reduce to reality the pictures of universal devotion to England and English interests." The political sentiments of the Irish "are generally identical with those of the Irish in the mother country." The French Canadians have "no feeling whatever for England." They are "governed by the priest with the occasional assistance of the notary."

The priests "put their interests into the hands of a political leader, who makes terms for them and for himself at Ottawa, and as the priests are reactionists, Canada has long witnessed the singular spectacle of Roman Catholics and Orangemen marching together to the poll." While, in the passages to which I have adverted, the writer deducts the French and Irish elements from the loyal portion of the population, he in his "enumeration of the forces which make in favour of the present connexion, leads off with the "reactionary tendencies of the priesthood which leads French Canada, and which fears that any change might disturb its solitary reign." It is true that the essayist makes a "forecast" that "the ice will melt at last;" but I am much mistaken if the Roman Catholic clergy will not smile with derision at the idea that one of the agencies is to be "the leaven of American sentiment brought back by French Canadians who have sojourned as artisans in the States," the other being "the ecclesiastical aggressiveness of the Jesuits." I shall not discuss the alleged "struggle for ascendancy between the Jesuits and the Gallicans," but shall merely observe that if any such struggle is going on, the contending parties contrive not to trouble their neighbours of other denominations with their controversies. The point of interest is, whether the French Canadians and the Irish are satisfied with their present government, and the essayist, although classing them as disloyal, is compelled to admit that at present they are adverse to change, and he can only rest his hopes on his own "forecast of the future." I have said that there was an error as to fact in this portion of the essay. It is not true that the Irish Catholic vote has of late been with the Conservatives. On the contrary, it is notorious that many elections in Ontario were carried for the Reformers by the Catholic vote. I am not aware how many Irish Catholics are in the House of Commons at present, but most assuredly Mr. Speaker Anglin and Mr. Devlin, M.P. for Montreal Centre, are representative Irish Catholics, and both are decided Liberals. Mr. Devlin contested Montreal Centre with an Irish Roman Catholic who ran in the Conservative interest, and he succeeded in obtaining a majority in a constituency in which, beyond all others, Irish Catholic influence prevails. And I may here observe that with reference to the remark "that the political sentiments of the Irish are identical with those of the Irish in the mother country," that it evinces a very superficial knowledge

THE POLITICAL DESTINY OF CANADA.

of the state of Irish feeling. I have shown how widely the Irish Catholics of Montreal differ as to Canadian politics; but it is nevertheless a fact that those same parties can unite in expressing opinions favourable to Home rule. The truth is that they are so attached to Home rule in Canada, that they would like, if possible, to see it extended to Ireland. Their sympathy with their fellow-countrymen in Ireland is manifested by pecuniary contributions; but with regard to Canadian politics they vote, not as a religious body, but according to the bias of their feelings and the various influences brought to bear on them. A sagacious statesman will at once perceive, what has completely escaped the observation of the essayist, that there is no inconsistency whatever in the Irish Catholics in Canada being dissatisfied with the existing relations between Great Britain and Ireland, and yet being perfectly satisfied with those between the United Kingdom and Canada. The French Canadian Roman Catholics are likewise very far from unanimous in their political sentiments. There are two distinct parties, Conservative and Liberal,[1] and although the former is in the majority in the Province of Quebec, there is a minority, respectable both in numbers and talent; while in the

Dominion Liberal government there are three Cabinet Ministers, all Roman Catholics.

I shall now proceed to the third division of my criticism, viz: "erroneous reasoning." I entirely dissent from the position laid down at the opening of the essay, that it is wise or profitable for a statesman to regulate his policy by any "forecast of the future." Let me not be misunderstood. A wise statesman ought to endeavour to make the political institutions of his country as perfect as possible. If our statesmen in 1830 believed, as no doubt they did, that there was danger of revolution unless the representative system was reformed, it was their duty to apply a remedy. The same remark would apply to those statesmen who proposed and carried Catholic emancipation. But that is just what the essayist objects to, when he remarks that "party politicians cannot afford to see beyond the hour." He requires a "forecast of the future," which is precisely what neither he nor any other man is capable of making. It is said by the essayist that "to tax forecast with revolutionary designs or tendencies is absurd." To this I demur. Nothing is easier than for one who desires revolution, "to cast a political horoscope," to make a "forecast," and then, on the pretence of providing for what is certain to occur, to strain every effort to bring about the desired result. I am opposed to revolution, and if I could forecast anything in the future likely to bring it about, I would spare no effort to prevent it. The truth is that with the essayist "the wish is father to the thought." He evidently prefers the Republican system of Government to the Monarchical, at which he sneers incessantly throughout his essay. He seems, however, to give it a preference as being less democratic. He pronounces Canada "a democracy of the most pronounced kind;" considers the Governor-General "not wrong in saying that she is more democratic than the United States, where the President is an Elective King, and where the Senate, which though elective is Conservative, possesses great power, whereas the nominated Senate of Canada is a cypher." I may remark *en passant* that this same cypher threw out a ministerial bill of considerable importance passed by the Commons with reference to British Columbia, and that the Prime Minister made a distinct proposition to have that body increased in order to bring it more into harmony with the Commons. To return from this digression: "Demagogism and the other pests of democratic institutions are not to be conjured away by forms and phrases." "The Governor-General has formally avowed himself a *faineant*," which simply means that he has acted as the representative of a Constitutional Sovereign, instead of, as the essayist would have wished him to do, like "an Elective King." People are generally wise after an event. I have no doubt that many of the present Government party who were dissatisfied with Lord Dufferin's course during the political crisis of 1873, are now satisfied that it was the wisest he could have adopted. Had he refused to follow the advice of his Ministers, as to the prorogation of Parliament, and thus forced them to resign, he would no doubt have been more popular with their opponents, but he would not have enjoyed that universal respect which is felt towards him at present. Differing entirely as I do from the essayist as to the merits of the English system of Parliamentary Government and the Republican system of the United States, I cannot look with indifference on the attempt which he has made to influence English public opinion to force Canada into the American Union on the plea that it is her manifest destiny. One who admits that self-government is independence, and that such self-government Canada enjoys, can have no other object, in advocating, first Canadian nationality or independence, and, on the utter rejection of his proposals, then annexation to the United States, than to substitute for the British system of party government, the Republican Elective King, with Ministers not holding seats in the Legislature, and responsible only to their chief. Nothing is more easy than to point out the evils in party government, but it is wholly irreconcileable with fact to maintain that corruption is more prevalent under the Monarchical than under the Republican system. It is now some sixty years since a venerable living statesman, Earl Russell, treated the subject of party government with great ability. Among its bad effects he admitted the want of candour which it necessarily produces, party politicians, in the heat of controversy, being prone to attribute to their opponents intentions and motives of which they are as incapable as themselves. Moreover, there is a tendency in politicians, even when convinced of an error, to adhere to wrong views rather than afford a triumph to their opponents. With regard to the corruption, Earl Russell maintains strongly that party connection is a great safeguard against it. I hope to be excused giving a short extract from the French edition of Lord Russell's work, which is the only one within my reach:—"En reconnaissant les mauvais effets des partis, je n'ai rien dit des animosités et des querelles violentes qu'ils suscitent. D'hypocrites philosophes, des femmes sentimentales, des hommes efféminés, ne cessent de se livrer à des lamentations sur les divisions politiques et les élections contestées. Les hommes d'un esprit élevé savent qu'elles sont les signes de la liberté et de la prosperité de la nation. C'est dans la chaleur et sous le marteau de l'enclume que la liberté acquiert ses formes, sa trempe, et sa vigueur."* I believe that I express the views of Canadians of all parties in affirming the great superiority of the British system of Parliamentary Government over the Republican system which the Canadians have ample opportunity of contrasting with their own. I have never been able to satisfy myself that we can enjoy that system of government except as a dependency of

---

* The following is the passage in the original English edition: "In reckoning up the bad effects of party, I have not spoken of the animosities and violent contentions it produces. Mock philosophers, sentimental women, and effeminate men are always making lamentations over political divisions and contested elections. Men of noble minds know that they are the workshop of national liberty and national prosperity. It is from the heat and hammering of the smithy that freedom receives its shape, its temper, and its strength.

the crown of England, and I therefore unhesitatingly avow that I am in favour of perpetual connection, although I am ready to admit that circumstances may lead to a revolution in any State or Kingdom or Empire.

The essayist, in order to establish the correctness of his forecast of the future insists that what he calls "the great forces" must prevail over "the secondary forces" which he admits may suspend the action of the great forces. In my judgment he has wholly omitted from his calculations the greatest force of all, viz., the reluctance of the people of any country to engage in revolutionary proceedings, which reluctance can only be overcome when some intolerable grievance exists, for which no other remedy but revolution can be found. I am unaware of any case in which a political revolution involving a change of allegiance has taken place without civil war, and I am firmly persuaded that such a revolution would not take place in Canada without the occurrence of that fearful calamity. I am well aware that when the subject is discussed by English politicians, they invariably assume that any controversy which may arise in the future will be between England and Canada, the Canadian people being supposed to be a unit. This is a most serious mistake. Judging from the state of public opinion in Canada, and I am unaware of any other mode of forming a judgment on the point, there is no probability whatever that Canadians will be united in favour of any revolutionary change. They are united at present in favour of the connexion with Great Britain, and so long as the advocates of revolution content themselves with writing essays in the *Fortnightly*, and avoid obtruding their opinions in Parliament or at the hustings, the loyalists will probably treat them with silent contempt. Should, however, any serious revolutionary movement be attempted, what are termed "the secondary forces" would most assuredly display the same vigour that they have done on previous occasions.

I must, however, ask attention to what the essayist terms the great forces which must in his opinion prevail. They are, 1st, distance; 2nd, divergence of interest; 3rd, divergence of political character; 4th, the attractive force of the great American community which inhabits the adjoining territory. Now, after a calm consideration of all that the essayist has said to prove that these are "great forces," I must confess that I have failed to find more than a single obstacle to the permanency of the connexion. On the question of distance the essayist argues that "political institutions must after all bear some relation to Nature and to practical convenience. Few have fought against geography and prevailed." Again, he says that the distance "can hardly be much shortened for the purposes of representative government." I confess that unless the foregoing language has some reference to the Pan-Britannic system, I fail to comprehend it. In the first ten years of Confederation the distance has not been found in the slightest degree inconvenient, and I can conceive no reason why it should be in the future. 2nd. Divergence of interest. It is contended that Englishmen control the foreign policy of the Empire, and having no interest in those questions in which Canada is chiefly interested, "betray by the languor of their diplomacy, and the ease with which they yield, their comparative indifference." No doubt there have been three or four occasions on which Canada has been dissatisfied with British diplomacy. I am not aware of any treaty made by England since the Treaty of Utrecht, in the reign of Queen Anne, that has not been vigorously attacked by the Opposition of the day. When the representatives of contending powers come to treat, they each find it absolutely necessary to make concessions, and such concessions always cause dissatisfaction. It may, however, be assumed that, as a rule, the British Government has endeavoured to select diplomatists of experience and ability to conduct their negotiations, and that their representatives are better informed as to what it is expedient to press than those who criticize their acts. It is, however, unfortunate for the argument of the essayist that although our boundary questions have been always settled unsatisfactorily according to our judgment, no feeling of disloyalty to England has been manifested in consequence. I think therefore that, notwithstanding the fact that there may be some divergence of interest, if it has led to no feeling of disloyalty in the past, it is still less likely to do so in the future. It is alleged by the essayist, not only that the interests of the Canadians are neglected owing to the apathy evinced by English statesmen in questions of controversy between Canada and the United States, but likewise that Canadians run the risk of being involved in war without having any voice in the preceding deliberations. It is now upwards of twenty years since I published a pamphlet in London, in reply to a very similar complaint. I shall venture to make a quotation from it:

THE POLITICAL DESTINY OF CANADA.

"The next complaint is that the interest of the colonies may be seriously affected by the decision of the mother-country to engage in war, and yet they are not consulted on the subject. It may be admitted as a possible contingency that the mother-country might engage in war on grounds which would be deemed insufficient in the colonies, and that if the property of the latter were exposed to loss or injury in consequence, disaffection might ensue. I am, however, of opinion that nothing can be more unprofitable than speculating on contingencies which may never arise. It is a far more probable contingency that the mother-country might be compelled to engage in war to protect one of her colonies, as she has been lately to protect an ally from a powerful oppressor. The colonies cannot be consulted about the question of war, because they contribute nothing to the expense of it, and would, in my opinion, be very sorry to purchase the privilege of being consulted at the price of bearing a just share of the burden. It is worthy of remark here, that the last war with the United States arose from a dispute on a question in which the North American Provinces had little or no interest. It was clear that the Canadians would be the principal sufferers, and it was imagined that they would be too glad to purchase tranquillity at the price of their allegiance. But the result proved that the British and French Canadians rallied with equal promptitude round the national standard, and the militia of the provinces, with very little assistance from the regular army, was strong enough to expel the invaders. With such a precedent I have no apprehension that the relations now subsisting between the mother-country and the colonies would be disturbed by the engagement of the former in a just

108 THE POLITICAL DESTINY OF CANADA.

war, and I do not believe in the probability of its engagement in an unjust one."

The 3rd great force, said to be "more momentous still," is the "divergence of political character." Under this the essayist descants on aristocracy, the Anglican Church, custom of primogeniture, militarism, &c., &c. The simple answer is, that England makes no attempt whatever to introduce into Canada any of her peculiar institutions or customs, and there has never been the slightest difficulty between the two governments growing out of divergence of political character. The fourth great force is "sure in the end" to be attractive, but not a shadow of an argument is adduced to support the assertion except a vague reference to "commercial influences," already discussed under the second head of "divergence of interest." This is the single difficulty, for it must be admitted that, if it were practicable, the abolition of the frontier custom-houses would be beneficial to both countries. The question is not one that could be conveniently discussed on such an occasion as this, but hitherto the effect of discussing measures of commercial policy with the United States has not been either to induce Canadians to admire the institutions of their neighbours, or to be attracted towards them in any way.

While the " great forces" are so little likely to lead the Canadian people to engage in revolutionary projects, the essayist has enumerated a number of secondary forces, all sufficiently powerful at present to account for the loyalty of the people, but, in his opinion, "of a transient character." These are as follows—1st. The French Canadians are led by their priests, who are at present satisfied, but then in the future the ice will melt under the influence of the Jesuits and "the leaven of American sentiment brought back by artizans." 2nd. United Empire Loyalists are in the position of the Jacobites after the extinction of the House of Stuart, but all their loyalty has evaporated since the English Ambassador saluted the American flag " in the celebration of the Centenary." 3rd. English emigrants are rapidly decreasing, and " as they die off natives take their places, so that Canada will soon be in Canadian hands." 4th. The social influence of the British officers has ceased with the military occupation. I learn for the first time, to my great surprise, though I was not without opportunity of forming a correct judgment, that these officers "exercised a somewhat tyrannical influence over opinion."

5th. The Anglican Church still fosters loyalty, but its roots "do not appear to be strong;" it is rent by the conflict between the Protestants and the Ritualists, and "discord has already taken the form of disruption." Now I should admit the appositeness of this argument, if it could be shown that either the Protestants, as they are called, or the Ritualists, or the members of the Reformed Church, were disloyal; but inasmuch as they are all equally loyal to the crown, I can conceive no reason for referring in this connexion to the differences as to ritualism. The connexion of Canadian Methodism with the States is said to be "very close," but it has never to my knowledge had the effect of making the members of that influential body disloyal to the crown. 6th. It is admitted that Orangeism is "strong in British Canada," but it is hoped that "one day" Orangeism must die. Of one thing the essayist may be assured, and that is, that should any attempt be made to promote a revolution the Orangemen will be ready to fight to the last in support of the connexion with the Crown of Great Britain. 7th. The social influence of English aristocracy, and of the little court of Ottawa. I presume this has reference to the Representative of the Crown, for the English aristocracy most assuredly do not seek to exert influence in Canada. 8th. Antipathy to the Americans. 9th. The special attachment felt by the politicians to the present system. Some of these secondary forces are wholly unworthy of notice, while others are infinitely more powerful than the greater forces, and others again are wholly omitted. Surely, in a country where the Scotch exercise so large an influence, where the First Minister is of that nation, as well as many members of both Houses of Parliament, their force is worthy of notice. I have no doubt that it would be, as it has ever been, with the loyalists. It does not appear, indeed, that there is any discontented class, for I have already shown that the French Canadians and the Irish Catholics are perfectly satisfied with the institutions under which they live. The policy of a true Canadian statesman is to endeavour, in the improbable event of any cause of difficulty arising between the Imperial and Canadian Governments, by every means in his power to remove it.

The essayist displays most bitter hostility to Confederation, and, as usual with him, the responsibility for that measure is thrown on England. He argues that, while a "spontaneous confederation" develops mainly the principles of union, "a confederation brought about by external influence is apt to develop the principles of antagonism in at least an equal degree." He proceeds to state that if an appeal be made to the success of confederation in Switzerland, the answer is, that Switzerland is not a dependency but a nation. Now, as the writer has himself assured us that "self-government is independence," and as the Canadian Confederation has practically the same power as the Swiss, I am unable to discover how the control of its external relations tends to produce success. Those relations lead to complications and difficulties, but cannot in any way ensure the success of the domestic government. But surely the essayist must be well aware that no confederation could be more spontaneous than the Canadian one. It was most assuredly not brought about by external influence, unless in so far as Nova Scotia was concerned. It appears, however, that "the proper province of a Federal government is the management of external relations," and as "a dependency has no external relations," it is implied that "the chief duty of a Federal government in Canada is to keep itself in existence by the ordinary agencies of party, a duty which it discharges with a vengeance." There is a simple answer to all this. The powers of the Dominion Parliament and of the Local Legislatures are clearly defined in the Imperial Statute, and during the ten years that it has been in force, no serious difficulty has arisen. The essayist informs us that, "had the movement in favour of nationality succeeded, the first step would have been a legislative union." He admits that there would have been opposition to such a step on the part of Quebec, but this is no difficulty with an advanced liberal, for "Quebec, if she had been handled with determination, would most likely have given way." It is consolatory to find that, although our political horoscope has been cast, it is admitted that "to specify the time at which a political event will take place is hardly ever possible," and it is further admitted that there is "a real complication of secondary forces," in other words, the secondary forces are all at present loyal to the core: but then there may be a continuance of commercial depression in Canada accompanied by prosperity in the United States; then there may be financial difficulties in Canada owing to the Pacific railway, in short something may occur. "A critical moment may arrive, and the politicians, recognising the voice of Destiny, may pass in a moment to the side of continental union." I will close these remarks by repeating what I have already stated, that I do not believe in the probability of a complete change of allegiance being brought about in any other way than as the result of a civil war, a calamity so fearful that it will not be hazarded unless some serious misunderstanding should arise between the two governments, and I cannot conceive that any such contingency is at all probable.

REMARKS

ON THE

CRITICISMS OF SIR FRANCIS HINCKS.

The position, experience and ability of Sir Francis Hincks afford a sufficient assurance that the case on his side will have been fully and well set forth. I think I may venture to add, that he has shown no unwillingness to expose any error or false reasoning of mine. The critical tendency has been displayed with still less reserve in other articles ascribed to his pen; and he seems even inclined to applaud and by applauding to adopt, abuse which I should have thought a lover of honourable controversy would disdain. He not seldom appeals to prejudice against me as a Liberal; but before taunts on that subject can come with propriety from his pen, the sponge must be passed over a great part of his own career. If I have yet seen no reason for deserting my principles, that surely is no disgrace.

My critic begins by quoting largely from a sermon preached by a clergyman of the Anglican Church before the St. George's Society of Montreal, in which he appears to himself to find a trustworthy index to the political sentiment of the future. The preacher is personally entitled to the highest respect; but when I am told that he is in no sense a party politician, I must answer that the Church which he represents is itself a political party. It has been throughout its history as much of a political party as of a church. In the doubtful region where it has hovered between Catholicism and Protestantism, between private judgment and priestly authority, while it has not been very steadfast in its adherence to any distinctive system of doctrine, it has been very steadfast in its adherence to the cause of political reaction. It has taken an active part in all the great attempts to overthrow English liberty. It has been the oracle of Divine Right and passive obedience. In English elections, at the present day it is of all the allies of Toryism the staunchest as well as the most powerful. The organic principles, the tendencies, the hopes, of society on this continent are utterly alien to it. A land without a connection between church and state, without a privileged religion, without bishops in the House of Lords, without a Defender of the Faith, without a congenial aristocracy to support clerical influence, must seem to it, spiritually and politically, out of the way of grace. It longs to bring back the New World under salutary bondage to the Old World, as the most energetic and probably the most numerous section of its clergy longs and strives to bring back society altogether to the salutary superstitions of the Middle Ages. I gave it what seemed its proper place among the secondary forces which work for the continuance of the present connection, observing at the same time that it seemed likely to be broken up by internal differences of opinion on fundamental questions, which are every day becoming more pronounced and more violent in their manifestations. Sir Francis Hincks says that disruption would not signify, because all the fragments would be loyal. It may perhaps be doubted whether the Protestant or Rationalist is exactly on a level with the Ritualist in the mental tendencies which Sir Francis Hincks would call loyal. But I spoke of the influence of Anglicanism as an organized body ; and the influence of an organized body would surely be impaired by its dissolution.

In private, perhaps, one who may justly claim a place among " sagacious politicians," would be ready to admit that as a key to the future state of sentiment and the probable course of future events in a community of the New World, a sermon preached by an Anglican clergyman before a congregation of English immigrants was little more significant than a saying of King George III.

Sir Francis Hincks undertakes to convict me (1) of errors of fact, (2) of inconsistencies, (3) of erroneous reasoning.

The errors of fact, ushered in as though they were many and grave, turn out to be in number two, both relating to secondary points and to matters less of positive fact than of impression. In the first of the two cases, however, Sir Francis Hincks has misconstrued me. I did not cite the Intercolonial and Pacific Railways as instances of the interference, much less of the unwarrantable interference. of the Colonial office with our public works. I cited them as instances of the influence of the Imperial connection in prompting us to undertakings from which, if we were guided only by our own interests and our own councils, wisdom might teach us to abstain. The Imperial character of the two works will scarcely be disputed when each has received an Imperial guarantee. It will scarcely be disputed either that both of them are rather political and military than commercial. As a merely commercial enterprise the Intercolonial would not do much credit to the sagacity of the projectors, since in addition to the sum spent in its construction it is run and seems likely to be run at an annual loss. Of the Pacific, as everybody seems to admit, the main object is to link together provinces at opposite sides of the Continent, because they fall within a line traced by the hand of empire, not by the hand of nature nor by any hand which had nature for its guide. " My *bête noire* " the Pacific Railway is not, and in calling it so, Sir Francis Hincks shows a tendency which is displayed throughout his paper, to exaggerate the position of his opponent for the purpose of giving effect to his reply; but it seems to be something like the *bête noire* of a good many Canadian politicians, for Sir Francis himself tells us that it has been "a subject of unceasing reproach by each political party against its antagonists;" so that either half the public men of Canada are very factious, or I have said nothing very absurd.

The second error of fact with which I am charged is in tracing the policy of annexing Manitoba and British Columbia to the Colonial Secretaryship of Sir Bulwer Lytton. My expression was, perhaps, not so precise as it ought to have been; but I meant to refer to the origin, not to the legislative consummation of the scheme. That the legislative consummation came later, nobody who has witnessed the controversies of the last six years about the treaty with British Columbia and the Pacific Railway questions could possibly fail to be aware. If Sir Bulwer Lytton was not the father of the scheme he got the credit of being so, and it was one likely to spring from his lively and ambitious fancy. But Sir Francis Hincks knows best. I can well afford to dispense with the illustration, for an illustration it was and nothing more. Examples are not wanting of British statesmen made Colonial Secretaries on grounds of party convenience rather than of personal aptitude, and called upon without knowledge or with only the knowledge picked up from Under-Secretaries or Colonial frequenters of the Office to decide upon measures vital to the welfare of young nations. With the Pacific Railway I have in no way connected Sir Bulwer Lytton's name.

2. The inconsistencies with which I am charged so far as I can see (and I must own the medium is not very pellucid) are three. The first is in some of my statements respecting the government of dependencies. But I must confess that after

THE POLITICAL DESTINY OF CANADA. 121

carefully perusing and reperusing a long paragraph I fail to perceive the point of the indictment. I have said that political tutelage while it was really exercised was an evil. I have said that to exercise it now would be absurd, seeing that of the holders of political power in the imperial country the great mass, all indeed with very few exceptions, are too much occupied with their own concerns and too ill instructed about the colonies to form any opinion upon colonial questions. I have said that through successive concessions to the principle of self-government political tutelage has been tending to extinction. That these are three distinct statements is clear; it is clear also that each of them is unpalatable to Sir Francis Hincks; but how they contradict each other I entirely fail to apprehend.

That the same language is not applicable to the colonial system in the different stages of its existence, is a fact of which I could hardly be ignorant, since I took part in the discussion which led to the last great change.

The same language is not applicable to the colonial system in the different stages of its existence, nor is the same language applicable to the different portions of it now. Of political self-government almost a full measure has been conceded, and unless the English Tories, emboldened by the appearance of reaction, should attempt to resume any of the prerogatives granted away by their Liberal predecessors, it is difficult to imagine the occurrence of a serious disagreement on that ground. But our commercial autonomy is doubtful; by some it is denied; and at any rate we still bear the commercial burden of the connection in being partly excluded, as a dependency of England, from the markets of other nations, above all from those of the United States, whereby we pay a heavy tribute, not in money, but in sacrifice of prosperity, to the Imperial nation. And so with regard to foreign relations generally, the position of the dependency remains unchanged; we are as liable as ever to be drawn by the Mother Country into war; she is as liable as ever to be drawn into war by us; and we are in principle as liable as ever to be called upon to contribute o Imperial armaments, though our payments would be levied and our contingents raised through a Parliament of our own.

My second inconsistency is in saying that there are no questions great enough to divide parties in Canada, and that consequently party government here is out of place; whereas, says my critic, I mention in the course of my essay some questions which an "experienced politician" would deem important enough to form dividing lines. I am inconsistent in short, not with myself, but with Sir Francis Hincks; a new version of inconsistency. The questions upon which Sir Francis Hincks fixes are Protection and the Pacific Railway. Protection can hardly be called a political question at all: here as in the United States the line of division between Protectionists and Free Traders crosses the line of division between political parties; in this country it crosses the party division in the case of Sir Francis Hincks, who, it seems, is a Conservative but a Free Trader. As to the question of the Pacific Railway, the idea of dividing our people into parties upon it, and making it the test of fitness to govern the country, so far from being mine, or available for the purposes of an indictment against my consistency, seems to me when propounded to be as untenable as anything can be.

What I said was that " party government was the bane of Canada." Sir Francis Hincks, in referring to my words, substitutes "Parliamentary" for " party." Is this fair? Is it fair to affect surprise " that so advanced a Liberal as the essayist should be an extreme Protectionist," when the fact is that I have simply referred to the existence of a protectionist movement without myself expressing any opinion on the subject. I am as far as my critic is from being a Protectionist, though I deem it frivolous to talk of upholding the principle of Free Trade, while we submit, for the sake of a political object (whether sufficient or insufficient is another question), to exclusion from the markets of the continent of which we are and cannot help being economically a part. Free Trade is the course of nature. The political connection which identifies Canada with a country in the other hemisphere and cuts her off from her own is as contrary to the course of nature as any thing that the most extreme Protectionist could devise.

It does not follow from my denying the excellence of party government in a country where there are no rational grounds for the existence of parties, that I must wish to introduce an elective Presidency and a Cabinet without seats in Parliament. I have more than once ventured to suggest that the elective presidency of the United States is a questionable reproduction of the monarchy of the Old World; that the periodical elections tend, among other evils, to bring public questions to a dangerous head, as they did in the fatal case of slavery; and that an Executive

Council elected, with a proper system of rotation, by the legislature would probably be the better plan. The machinery of democratic government was framed under misleading influences; it is still very imperfect, and there is room for hope that some of the evils of democracy may be diminished by removing these mechanical defects. But the English system can have no place in Canada. A balance of power between Estates is impossible where there is no Estate but the Commons; and Party, to which in England reason enough for existence is supplied by the conflict, still undecided, between aristocracy and democracy, is without a reason for its existence here. Sir Francis Hincks admits as much when he sets to work to provide the Canadian parties with a new principle of division, and after boxing the compass hesitates at last between Protection and the Pacific Railway. Party, without great questions, is faction; and faction, if it is not checked, will before long bring calamities on the country. Sir Francis Hincks knows the meaning of the scene before him, though he speaks of it with faltering lips. He calls my remarks indiscriminate because they apply equally to both parties; as though one party could have a dividing line when the other had none. The character of all factions, in the same country, is pretty sure to be the same. Lord Russell's defence of party, to which Sir Francis Hincks appeals, applied to a country in which the parties have a meaning. And why does Sir Francis Hincks pride himself upon being unconnected with either party, after having tried both, if party in this country is a good thing?

The third charge of inconsistency has reference to the account I have given of the different sentiments prevailing in the different sections, national and religious, of our people. And here again I have to confess that the subtlety of the accusation eludes the grasp of my simple understanding. Where is the inconsistency of saying that the priesthood of Quebec is opposed to union with the States from motives of sacerdotal conservatism, and at the same time that the French population of the Province "is not devoted to England and English interests"? This, I beg leave to observe, was my expression, though Sir Francis Hincks finds it convenient for his argument and for the impression which he wishes to create to insert the term "disloyal." It is interesting to find that in the remote seclusion of Montreal, Sir Francis Hincks has heard nothing of any struggle for ascendancy between the Jesuits and their Gallican opponents. "If," he says, " any such struggle is going on, the contending parties contrive not to trouble their neighbours of other denominations with their controversies." From his paper we should almost gather that he was unaware of any disturbance of the harmony which reigns around him by quarrels between Roman Catholics and Orangemen, though the fact has since been brought under his notice. Of the Irish sentiment, his explanation is one which he justly observes, has escaped the observation of a poor essayist, and could be discerned only by "a sagacious statesman." "The truth is," he says, "that the Irish are so attached to Home Rule in Canada that they would like, if possible, to see it extended to Ireland." This their loyal and affectionate aspiration finds singular expression in the columns of their favourite journals. That the Irish Catholics are not exclusively and inflexibly attached to either of the Canadian parties, is a fact of which we have abundant proof in the political flirtations which are going on around us; but it tells us nothing as to their feelings with regard to British connection. A Conservative politician would not reject a vote, or refrain from trying to secure it, because the voter was a Fenian, any more than a Presbyterian politician rejects a vote or refrains from soliciting it because the voter is a Papist. I trust I shall not go beyond the mark in saying that the picture of Canadian sentiment drawn by Sir Francis Hincks is somewhat official, and that an English statesman who should accept it without misgiving, as an English statesman is warranted in accepting anything from Sir Francis Hincks, would not be entirely in possession of the actual facts.

3. Erroneous Reasoning. Under this head we expect to find instances of a want of proper connection between premises and conclusion. But in the vocabulary of Sir Francis Hincks erroneous reasoning seems to mean the expression of opinions in which he does not concur. I have submitted, as a justification for the subject of my essay, that statesmen engaged in building up the institutions and forming the character of a young nation will be aided, not embarrassed, by a true forecast of its political destiny. From this proposition, Sir Francis Hincks " entirely dissents," though not without showing himself conscious that an explanation of his dissent may be required. But his dissent is no proof of any want of connection between my premises and the not very paradoxical conclusion at which I arrived. A want of logical connection there might have been if instead of statesman I had said politician.

Even a politician, however, must be rather an extreme specimen of the class, if he can go on draining the resources of a not very wealthy country to construct a separate system of political and military railroads, without caring to inquire what the political and military relations of the country in the future are to be. He must be rather an extreme specimen of his class if he can go on legislating for Canadian industry and commerce, without caring to inquire in what channels they are destined to run. The reflection extends in a certain measure to all military expenditure, to money given out of Canadian resources in aid of emigration to the far West, and to the annual outlay of a large sum on public works in British Columbia.

To a string of miscellaneous contradictions, unsupported by argument, I hardly know what answer to make. I can only say that I have given, to the best of my ability, my reasons for my opinions, and that when new arguments are brought before me, my opinions shall be reconsidered. To one or two of the questions here cursorily mooted by Sir Francis Hincks, I may advert before I have done.

We find ourselves approaching the end of Sir Francis Hincks' paper before we come to the real point. My essay is an attempt to forecast the political destiny of Canada by a method the soundness of which experience has proved. I endeavour to distinguish the great and permanent forces from those which are secondary in strength or transient, assuming that, however numerous, and however complex the secondary forces may be, the great forces will in the end prevail. I have enumerated four forces which seem to me to be great, all of them tending to the ultimate severance of the political connection (it is of the political connection alone that I speak), between Canada and the Old World. The four are distance, divergence of interest, divergence of political character, and the attraction of the great mass of English-speaking people which adjoins us on this continent. The first three are passed over by Sir Francis Hincks, with a few curt and somewhat supercilious remarks, the upshot of which is that as these forces have never caused disloyalty in the past, they are not likely to cause it in the future. Some of them, being neglected by unwise politicians, did cause the American Revolution, and what may almost be called a revolution in Canada. But who talks of disloyalty? Not I, but Sir Francis Hincks. I should as soon think of taxing the natural succession of the seasons with disloyalty, as the natural course of political progress, tending towards an end, which, so far as we can see, is good. If Sir Francis Hincks chooses to hold the greater force guilty of disloyalty for preponderating over the lesser, he must be allowed to do so; but for my part I wish to adhere to the rules of common sense and calmly to consider the probabilities of the future, as they result from past experience and present facts. Distance, divergence of political character and divergence of interest, operating in the past, have led in the case of the United States, to a complete political separation from the Mother Country; in the case of Canada to that large measure of political separation which is called self-government, as well as to the practical rejection up to this time of hereditary aristocracy, the abolition of the Church Establishment, and the adoption of a tariff, which takes us out of the commercial unity of the Empire, though it may not imply that we are in possession of complete commercial autonomy. It may be that these forces in the case of Canada are exhausted, and that so far as our political relations with the Mother Country are concerned, we have arrived at our final state. Let Sir Francis Hincks prove this or show that it is probable and I am answered. But at present he is merely rending his garments and throwing dust into the air.

I pointed to the feebleness of England's diplomacy on this Continent as proving the faintness of her interest. Sir Francis Hincks replies that all treaties made by governments, from the Treaty of Utrecht downwards have been attacked by the Opposition. But the strongest objections to the treaties by which Canadian interests were sacrificed did not come from the English Opposition; they came from Canada. Does Sir Francis Hincks mean to say that the objections to the Oregon Treaty were mere party objections? I know the Oregon treaty did not make us "disloyal" any more than it made us lame or bald, but it did show that England felt her interests to be anything but identical with those of Canada; and where interests are not identical political union is apt not to be lasting.

War made by England for an object in which Canada had no concern would place the divergence of interest in a strong light. Of this Sir Francis Hincks is aware; but he thinks to conjure away the difficulty by repeating from a pamphlet of his own the formula that England will never make an unjust war, and that in a just war Canada will not object to suffer. The war against the French

Republic, the war with the United States in 1812, the Crimean war are not regarded by all Englishmen as just, and the Lorcha war with China was voted unjust by the House of Commons. But a word on this point hereafter.

The fourth force is the attraction of our own Continent. In this, Sir Francis Hincks allows that there is something deserving his consideration, at least from the economical point of view. "This," he says, "is the single difficulty, for it must be admitted that if it were practicable, the abolition of the Custom houses would be beneficial to both countries." At last then he has come to an important point, one on which he is eminently qualified to give an opinion, and on which he would be heard with the greatest interest, especially at a moment when fiscal and commercial questions are pressing with no ordinary force upon the public mind. How does he deal with this point? He evades it altogether, and passes it by without a word, on the pretence that "it could not be conveniently discussed on such an occasion as this;" covering his retreat by an irrelevant appeal to the prejudice against American character and institutions! We should admire the courage of the stage manager, who when the expectant audience were looking for the entrance of Hamlet, could come before the scene and tell them that the part of Hamlet was omitted as it could not be conveniently introduced on such an occasion as the performance of the play.

But my critic tells me that I have omitted from my list the greatest force of all, which, in his opinion, is the reluctance of the people of any country to engage in revolutionary proceedings. "I am unaware," he says, "of any case in which a political revolution involving a change of allegiance has taken place without civil war, and I am firmly persuaded that such a revolution would not take place in Canada without the occurrence of that frightful calamity." If in his idea of political revolution the writer mentally includes civil war, as there seems reason to suspect, his statement is indisputable but at the same time unfruitful. He can hardly mean that a change of allegiance has never taken place without civil war. The history of Europe is full of changes of allegiance without civil war by cession, exchange, purchase, marriage of heiresses, division of inheritance. In our own time Neufchatel, the Ionian Islands, Savoy, Nice, Alaska, the Transvaal and Cyprus have changed their allegiance without civil war. There is apparently no law of nature any more than there is a principle of morality, which when two civilized and intelligent communities find that political independence would be for their mutual benefit, forbids them to separate without first making war upon each other. Nor are we bound altogether to overlook the teachings of experience. Sir Francis Hincks has in his mind the American Revolution. But England has plainly and repeatedly declared that she will not again be guilty of the folly which when the American Colonies were ripe for independence, compelled them to achieve it with revolutionary arms. Even at the time of the quarrel with America, the most clear-sighted Englishmen perceived, what all perceive now, that the struggle to keep a full-grown community in the leading strings of dependence, was a struggle against nature. "The power," said the *Times*, "which we desire to exercise is entirely a moral one, and strong or weak, the dependency which wishes to quit us has only solemnly to make up its mind to this effect." Such, it may safely be said is the settled policy of England, when England is in her normal mood. Even in the midst of a Conservative reaction, it would hardly be possible to drag the English people into a war for the purpose of preventing a British Colony from becoming a nation. If there is to be a civil war it must be one got up by Sir Francis Hincks and those who consider that it is contrary to principle to allow a British Colony to take out its freedom as a nation without bloodshed. He seems to gloat over the idea that any attempt to change the existing system, would be resisted by the Orangemen with arms. I will not say that it surprises me that a public man once liberal should wish to see the political destinies of Canada and of this continent, violently controlled by a power which is the offspring and perpetuation of an old Irish feud. But I have already said that under the influence of a humane and tolerant legislation, Orangeism is declining in Ireland; and that the Canadian branch is not likely to survive the tree out of which it grows. If the account which Sir Francis, since the publication of his paper, has given of Orangeism be true, if Orangeism aims at forcing the Canadian people to submit to the yoke of Protestant ascendancy, it is not unlikely to come to its end in a more sudden and violent way.

To my enumeration of the secondary forces, Sir Francis Hincks takes no serious exception; but he complains that I have left out the Scotch who, he says, have great political influence in Canada, and " would be as they have ever been with the loyalists." I do not doubt that Scotchmen would, like all good citizens, be on the side of the law. But looking to the part they have played in Canadian history, we should hardly rank them with the United-Empire Loyalists. Certain it is that in the political revolution by which the Crown was practically stripped of its powers, Scotchmen played a part which to strong royalists and to the representatives of Royalty seemed anything but loyal. That Scotch Presbyterians as a class are less inclined to independence than English Episcopalians, it would surely be a historical paradox to assert.

Whichever may be the side of good sense, the Scotch, unless they belie their history, will be found ultimately on that side.

By reference to Sir Francis Hincks' paper, my readers will be able to judge whether I have given a fair account of his reply. They will see, at the same time, what points and arguments he has passed over in silence, and thus measure the strength of his resolution to deal fully and fairly with the whole question.

The truth is, that if he attempted to deal fully and fairly with the whole question, he would find himself compelled to come over to my side. He says he " is not presumptuous enough to declare that the subsisting connexion must be perpetual." He is not presumptuous enough to declare that he thinks it likely to be perpetual. He is not presumptuous enough to declare that it is not sure to come to an end.

The real force of his reply lies, I fear, not in its reasonings, but in the suggestion, which runs through the whole of it, that those who differ from him on these questions are disloyal, revolutionists and conspirators. He is constantly appealing to the political cowardice created by a terrorism of opinion. And with all who have anything to hope or fear from politicians or their organs, with all who, careless of the future, merely wish to be on the side of what is at present dominant and orthodox, the appeal is sure to be effective.

We see now how difficult it is to get at the real sentiment of the people of this country, and how fallacious after all, the official estimate of it derived from its public manifestations, may be. Who will speak his mind when, if he fails to agree with Sir Francis Hincks he is to be branded as a traitor and threatened with Orange revolvers? In a recent debate in the English House of Commons, a member said he had been in Canada six years before, and had then found a good deal of what he misnamed disloyal feeling in the background. In the background, if anywhere it was sure to be. I have myself reason to believe that a man may be publicly assailed with the utmost virulence for his opinions, by writers who in private do not differ from him. I know also that a public man may think it necessary, for political purposes, to fall in with the prevailing sentiment, while in his own mind, he regards Annexation as the inevitable end. The English member of Parliament, if he kept his ear and his mind open, was at least as likely to get at the truth as Governors General holding their court or making their state tours. His report is, to say the least, not more incredible than reports which include the French and Irish in their flattering pictures of universal and enthusiastic devotion to the interests of Great Britain. Is it rash to infer from this sudden lavishness, after a period of parsimony, in the distribution of titles, and from other measures indicative of the same policy, that there may be a misgiving on the part of the Tory Government in England, as to the perfect agreement between the official representations and the real state of things?

For my own part I have formed the general impression that except when some special stimulant is applied, the feeling of attachment to the present system, if not weak, is for the most part not so strong but that a powerful pressure of interest might give opinion a new turn; and moreover, that there is a considerable difference between the feelings of the immigrants and those of the native Canadians, the immigrants being often proud individually of their British birth, which they feel gives them a sort of superiority over the natives. I suspect that among the more active-minded of the natives the fire of nationality kindled by confederation still smoulders in spite of all the efforts of loyal politicians to extinguish it, and that upon the appearance of a leader (an event certainly not very probable) it might again burst into a flame.

In another critique we were bravely challenged to try the question at the polls. That we should try at the polls a speculative question respecting the future destiny of the country, seems a somewhat grotesque proposal. It would be something like asking a constituency to decide by ballot the probable recurrence of a comet. But in whose hands really are the polls? In those of the people or in those of the party organizations? Would the managers allow a self-nominated candidate to go with an issue of his own choosing before the people, and freely to take their votes upon it? Sir Francis Hincks as an experienced politician must know that such a challenge is a mockery.

It seems time to ask ourselves in what loyalty really consists? Is there any sound principle of public morality which renders it criminal to contemplate, to propose, or to promote by legal means the political severance of a colony from its mother country, supposing separation to be good for both. It seems time, I say, that we should look this question in the face. It is folly, in any case, to let a shadow bar the path, or to allow bad citizens to clothe themselves with a fictitious virtue, and taint good citizens with a fictitious crime. The loudness with which loyalty is professed by certain lips is enough to suggest the necessity of investigating its claims to our veneration. We know that the name is capable of abuse. We know that it was abused by the political sharpers who the other day were oppressing and plundering the Southern States. We know that it has been abused by tyrants, who have always called slaves loyal and branded patriots with disloyalty. In its etymological sense loyalty might be predicated of every law-abiding citizen. But under the Feudal System it denoted the sentiment connected with personal allegiance. It was then no irrational emotion, but the cement, rational because necessary, of the peculiar institutions of the time. It had nothing in it servile, reactionary or savouring of later superstitions about Legitimacy and the Divine Right of Kings. It was hardly even dynastic. It did not hinder the framers of the Great Charter or the founders of the House of Commons from adopting bold measures of innovation when innovation seemed improvement. It did not hinder them even from changing their allegiance when they saw good reason for the change. But we are not living in the Middle Ages. The feudal doctrine of personal allegiance is not the basis of modern institutions. Naturalization laws and treaties have distinctly set it aside. It can no longer form the rule or the warrant of our political actions. It can no longer forbid us to do, or absolve us if we neglect to do, anything that is required by the common weal. It is superseded by the sentiments of duty to the State and devotion to the common good. He in whom those sentiments manifest their presence, who keeps all laws, obeys all constituted authorities, and seeks no change except by peaceful and legal means cannot, among freemen, be called disloyal.

If mere change of allegiance, or the contemplation of it, without any disposition to rebellion, is disloyalty, all the emigrants from Europe to the United States must be disloyal. All the persons of Canadian birth who have settled on the other side of the line must be disloyal. The present proprietors of the *Globe*, now Sir Francis Hincks' best allies, must have gone fearfully near the verge of disloyalty when they took up their residence as journalists in New York. The case of the mass of people collectively forming a colony does not appear, in this respect, to differ in principle from that of the individual emigrant. The conservative Lord Derby said in a speech, already cited, to the electors of King's Lynn, that Canada and Australia must, as everybody knew, soon become separate nations. Was Lord Derby disloyal himself, and a preacher of disloyalty to others?

In a more general sense loyalty means devotion to a public principle, whether it be the principle of legitimacy embodied in a particular dynasty, as in the case of the Jacobites, or one of a more modern and rational kind. A man may be said, in this sense to be loyal if, being a citizen of the New World, he is faithful to its social principles, to its hopes, to the apparent designs of Providence in thus leading up mankind out of the realms of feudalism and placing them on a Continent admirably fitted to be the scene of an ampler and happier development of humanity, to the people whose labour has won for themselves and for all of us here a land beyond the influence and traditions of Norman conquest. Loyalty of this kind may perhaps be soon put to the proof; for there is every appearance of a renewed effort on the part of aristocracy to propagate its influence and restore its ascendancy here. Sir Francis Hincks says that England "makes no attempt whatever to introduce into Canada any of her peculiar institutions or customs." Historically this is scarcely correct, since an hereditary peerage was projected, hereditary baronetcies were conferred, and the State Church of England was established and endowed, while orders of knighthood, though not hereditary, are more congenial, to say the least, to aristocratic than to democratic institutions. But the hope of fostering aristocratic sentiment and antagonism to American democracy has never been quite relinquished, and it has evidently been revived by the Conservative reaction in England, consequent on the influx of wealth, and by the reawakening of that spirit of military and territorial aggrandizement which is a part of the same movement. An imperialist and aristocratic policy (the two are, in the case of England, practically identical) is in the ascendant, and its operations are evidently about to be extended to the Colonies. Confederates, it is expected, will be found in Colonial wealth and in Colonial love of titles and social distinction. We are to be made instrumental, in common with the Empire of India, to the suppression of Liberalism in the Mother Country. But what the Tory aristocracy of England specially want of Canada is that she shall serve it as a political outpost, and interfere as much as possible with the consolidation of democratic institutions on this Continent. If Canada lends herself to that game she lends herself to her own ruin. She lends herself to her own ruin for the benefit, not of the Mother Country, but merely of the aristocratic party in it; for what the England of the people desires of the Colonies is only that they should make her the mother of free nations.

Aristocracy, not monarchy, is now the real power and the power against the designs of which those who are true to New World principles have to be on their guard. Constitutional monarchy is a mask prudently retained by aristocracy to hide features which, when actually displayed,

J

have seldom excited love. If the Royal prerogative were to be in any measure restored, it would be wielded by aristocratic hands in the interest of the order.

I am not so irrational as to be an enemy to monarchy in the abstract, nor have I "incessantly sneered at monarchical institutions throughout my essay," as Sir Francis Hincks in his usual style of invidious exaggeration asserts. I only say that hereditary government belongs to the Old World, and that if we rely on the hereditary principle as our safeguard against the dangers of democracy here, we shall be leaning on a bruised reed, and building on a frail foundation. Nay, even in the Old World, at least in the more civilized part of it, the hereditary principle appears to have arrived at its last stage of existence. In the East it still prevails in combination with other primitive customs and beliefs. It still prevails in half Asiatic Russia, where it is the necessity at once of a vastly extended empire and a race untrained in self-government. But in civilized Europe, one great nation has discarded it, while in the rest it lingers with greatly reduced prerogatives, and in several cases with a revolutionary title. Legitimacy is departing from the scene with the melancholy forms of the last Bourbons. To turn the eyes of the people here to the hereditary principle as the permanent basis of government and the security for social order, would be to disregard all the signs of the times. The only possible basis of government here is the national will; the only security for social order is the recognised justice and expediency of institutions. To purify the Republic of faction, demagogism, wirepulling, corruption and all the other evils by which thoughtful men see that it is fearfully beset, is no doubt a difficult task; but it is a noble task; it is a task in which public characters at least as high as any that present themselves in the history of monarchies may be formed; and it is the task allotted to us here. Here, apart from any republican cant we must be loyal to the people, to whom by right of labour this continent belongs; and we must show our loyalty to them not by pandering to their vanity and their passions, but by trying to make their reason and their morality prevail. Native Canadians will more readily admit this than Englishmen in whom the hereditary sentiment is ingrained, and who cannot fancy a government built securely on any other foundation. Yet we may all learn a lesson and take some comfort from the devotion with which the American people supported a government based on the national will during their great civil war.

Social influence the Crown still retains, though some of us have been carried by their loyalty to the verge of servility in tracing the morality of English men and English women to the beneficent example of a Court. Whether the social influence of the representative of the Crown in a colony is good depends not only on his personal qualities, but on the suitableness of the aristocratic model for our imitation, and the effect which an attempt to imitate it may have on the genuineness of our social character and the simplicity of our social life That the violence of political war is tempered and its coarseness refined by the presence of a British nobleman, is but a pleasing illusion as the records of the last session show. Neither at Ottawa nor at Westminster will the passion, which is generated by the fierce struggle for power and by the presence of hated antagonists, allow itself to be bridled by any silken thread. It would be wrong to say that the presence of a discreet and wellbred man of the world, with the prestige of rank, has not sometimes moderated the factious excesses of party leaders; but if we can find no surer antidote to faction than an influence of this sort, our political prospect is not fair.

Political inconsistency is always a venial fault; not seldom it is a virtue; but to warrant us in recognising it as a virtue some terms must be kept with the past. It is trying to patience to see men who have spent half their public lives in reducing the power of the Crown in a Colony to a shadow, turn round and denounce us as traitors because we cannot take the shadow for a substance and adopt it not only as the palladium of our political confidence, but as the object of a political religion. I did not arraign the decision of the Governor-General in the case of the Pacific Railway investigation, so that Sir Francis Hincks need not introduce that issue; but I said that his decision amounted to a total abnegation of real power, in other words to a declaration of faineancy. And this faineancy is the work of Reformers who are filled with loyal horror at the thought of any further change.

I perfectly understand the position of those who seeing, as every man of sense must see, the perils of democracy, wished to retain the reality of monarchical rule, especially as the power of the Crown in the case of a dependency was practically vested in a representative who could never be a George IV. It is not so easy to understand the position of those who having destroyed the reality make a desperate stand in defence of the name.

Attachment to England, to the England of the people, may surely be strong in a breast in which confidence in the hereditary principle of government is weak, and the love of aristocratic privilege till weaker. We, or at least the English portion of us, are bound to our mother country by ties of blood, history, language and literature, which would not snap with the attenuated thread of political connection. But we do not show ourselves the worthy offspring of England by want of self-reliance and self-respect. An English writer of note, the otherday, taking pity on the low estate of colonists, proposed to elevate them by the distribution among them of a few more pieces of ribbon or by the admission of a few of them to the professions of the mother country. It is always assumed that a Colony can have no honours or worthy objects of ambition in itself; and the assumption is too well justified by the bearing of many colonists and the language of many organs of colonial sentiment. Yet the people of the New World, those of English blood especially, have been picked out of the people of the Old World by a process of selection far higher and more searching than those which had determined the elements of any previous migration; by a process which combined religious and political aspiration with commercial enterprise, and which could hardly fail to bring to these shores the flower of the race. The qualities of self-government surely reside in the freeholders of Canada in as full a measure as in the tenant farmers of England or the masses of the English towns. In the products of industry our kinsmen in the United States are fast taking the first place among all nations. The historic glories of England belong alike to both branches of the race; and the American branch has in addition the history of an heroic colonization. Writers of Canadian history fill their pages with minute details of political strife or of border war. They leave untold, and soon they will have lost the traditional materials for telling, the most moving and instructive tale of all, that of the struggle with the wilderness. If no escutcheon can be bright without blood, surely blood and brave blood enough was shed in the war of 1812 and in the American Civil War. Culture and art of course come later, but in time they come; and manners are formed in the school of equality better in all essential respects than any that a representative of European privilege can teach.*

Sir Francis Hincks crows over the admission that the crisis of our destiny may yet be a long way off. It may be a very long way off, for aught I can tell. Its arrival depends on the course of events not only in Canada, England, and the United States, but in the world at large, for the partnership of nations and the sympathetic interaction of their politics become more manifest every day. But if Sir Francis Hincks will examine the cases of the unification of Germany, the liberation of Italy, the union between England and Scotland, to which I have referred, he will see that the event, long delayed, sometimes comes at last like a thief in the night. There is at present a Conservative and Imperialist reaction in England, which extends in some measure to the Colonies. But history is full of these backstreams. If the plethora of wealth and the other special causes to which the reaction is traceable, should cease to operate, the reaction itself would subside; England would return

---

* The social consequences of colonial self-prostration are what they might be expected to be. The author of the *Abode of Snow* has noticed the amusing way in which the social superiority of the Indian Service to colonists is asserted on board mail steamers.

to her normal mood ; moderation and sobriety of mind would resume their sway over her counsels; her people would again become conscious of the fact, which seemed to be dawning on them twenty years ago, that enormous and unnatural agglomerations of territory are not really and permanently conducive to wealth, strength or happiness. As it is, "Jingoism" is by no means universal in the mother country ; it is comparatively weak in the north of England, and has been almost entirely repelled by the good sense of Scotland. To the more clear-sighted it is already evident, that Imperialism is likely to bring as its penalty a loss or diminution of English liberty, and a corruption of the political character of the English people. But suppose Jingoism should prevail, and England should remain in her present frame of mind. Engrossed by Eastern aggrandizement, she may become less anxious to retain Western Colonies which contribute much to her military liabilities, and little to her military strength. There is yet a third contingency, not to be left altogether out of sight. Jingoism, like Chauvinism, arousing the natural jealousy and the just resentment of nations may, like Chauvinism, find its Sedan. In one way or other, the world, menaced by the ambition of aspirants to universal Empire, has always contrived to deliver itself in the end. Sir Francis Hincks trusts in sentiment, which, it is true, often lingers and rules the conduct of nations after the solid grounds for it have been removed. Still sentiment is not adamant, as even Canadian history will prove.

It is not likely that any political question will arise between the Colony and the Mother Country. This has been already admitted. But with regard to war, military expenditure and commercial autonomy it is not unlikely that serious questions may arise.

Sir Francis Hincks says that England will never get us into an unjust war. The England of the people will never get us into any war at all; for it is the England of industry, colonization and peace; nor is the England of the people in any way tempted to crusade against the political progress of other nations. It would not have made war upon the French Republic, and consequently it would not have involved Canada in the war of 1812. But the England with which we are likely to have to deal for the present is the England of the aristocracy, and the England of the aristocracy has twice within a few years brought Canada to the verge of war. It brought her to the verge of war for slavery, to which aristocracy was bound, both by the sympathy which unites privileged classes and by common enmity to the Republic, but which, had it triumphed by our aid, would have filled the veins of society on this continent with moral, political and industrial poison; and, again, the other day, for the maintenance within the borders of Christendom of Turkish despotism, with fatalism, slavery, polygamy and concubinage in its train. In both these cases the dependency would have been dragged, not only into suicidal folly, but into crime. The Anglo-Turkish convention may be described as a provision for a war, at no distant date, between England and Russia in Asia Minor; and the object of that war, even supposing justice to be on the side of England, would be so utterly remote from Canadian interests and obligations that to shed Canadian blood for them would be almost criminal.

War has been called the game of kings. It is equally the game of aristocracies, and not only their game but their natural policy. Apart from special objects of political propagandism or of territorial ambition, interest leads them to stimulate the military and imperial spirit as an antidote to thoughts which lead to political change.

Mr. Forster's fair vision of a Pacific British Empire has faded away. The British Empire stands revealed as an Empire, like other Empires, of military force. To that force all its members will probably be called upon to contribute, especially if, by their martial enthusiasm, they invite the demand. Even the peace party in England has an interest in enforcing the principle, because members who do not contribute, not feeling the burden, will be apt, in gaiety of heart, to applaud a spirited foreign policy, and to strengthen by their sympathy the hands of the war party in the Mother Country. But, when the call comes, the divergence of character between a military nation of the Old World and a commercial nation of the New World can hardly fail to appear. Canadians have shown that they are warlike enough in their own defence, but taxation for the maintenance of great standing armaments is one of the things to escape which many people have come here.

We of this generation do not know what war is. We might know if England were to provoke a hostile combination of maritime powers, as she one day will, if she is bent on making the Mediterranean a British Lake.

Commercial autonomy again is a question which can hardly fail soon to become practical, which in fact has become practical already. It is impossible that Canada should long remain content with the situation in which her industries are placed by the existing state of things. She cannot bear to have them at once excluded from their natural markets on this Continent and exposed to the crushing force of European and American competition. In the case of America indeed competition is not all; I am credibly informed at least that a sort of commercial war is waged by sending in American goods at a loss to prevent the development of certain manufactures in this country. This, it has already been said, is not free trade, nor is it a system which any English free trader can reasonably ask us to maintain. Our producers, placed under these artificial disadvantages by a political connection, naturally seek relief in some countervailing revision of the tariff. But when everything in the way of tariff revision has been tried, it will probably be found that the one thing needed, and the only effective remedy, is free access to the markets of our own continent. The abolition of the frontier custom houses between Canada and the United States is the policy to which, as Sir Francis Hincks allows, the common interest of both countries points. Nature beckons us to it with both hands. A special reciprocity treaty, supposing it could be negotiated, would be hardly worth having in comparison with a complete measure of continental free trade. It would not rid us of the expense and annoyance of the customs line; it would probably be unfair to some interests on both sides; it would be difficult of execution in regard to manufactures, because Canada could hardly be prevented from becoming an entrepot for European contraband; it would be precarious and liable to be overturned, with the industries built on it, by the first gust of anger between the nations: whereas a customs union would be in itself a strong cement of friendly relations, though it would not, any more than the postal union into which we have already entered, interfere in principle with political independence. But a customs union with the United States presupposes commercial autonomy; as indeed does any alteration of the tariff involving a large increase of the duties on European goods; and the commercial autonomy of the dependencies is not yet fully established, though large concessions to fiscal self-government have been made, and in the case of the Australian Colonies, there was some years ago almost a direct admission of the principle; an admission qualified in its practical bearing by the fact that at that time England was disposed to believe that the colonies injured only themselves by protection, whereas she is now more disposed to believe that they also injure her.

While these lines are passing through the press the London *Times* points out, that the dependencies being included in the commercial treaties made by the Imperial country, it is not in the power of England to permit any exercise of commercial autonomy by which the "most favoured nation" clauses or other stipulations of those treaties would be infringed. We are thus brought face to face with the fact that while the existing relations between the dependency and the Imperial country continue, the people of the dependency will be liable to having their commercial interests seriously affected by treaties in the negotiation of which they have no voice and which are probably framed almost exclusively with reference to the wishes of the people of the Imperial country. We are made sensible, in the most forcible manner, of the limited nature of the self-government which under the most liberal of colonial systems, a dependency can attain.

It is not to manufacturers alone that economical separation from our own continent is injurious. All Canadian property must be depreciated by that which arrests the natural flow of capital and commercial life. Cut off the most smiling section of England from the rest, and its aspect would soon be changed. Even property of little value in itself often acquires a high value by economical union with a wealthy country, as the moors and lochs of Scotland have acquired a high value by union with the wealth of England. Gifts, however gracious, will not restore the life of the past to the City of Quebec; but, economically united to the wealth of the continent, she might, with her beauty and her historic interests become the Edinburgh of America.

I am as fully persuaded as Sir Francis Hincks that the Conservative Protectionists of Canada deem their views consistent with their loyalty to the Crown; and I would at once recall any words of mine which I thought capable of conveying a contrary impression. No doubt it is against the United States immediately and mainly, not against British competition, that the Protectionism of our Conservatives is pointed. Still England is concerned, and the defeat of the Canadian Conservatives on the tariff resolution was a matter of rejoicing, as Sir Francis Hincks is aware, to all parties alike in the Imperial country. The commercial question must be pressing when it can force the Conservative party in this country to place itself in a position at all equivocal towards its political allies in Great Britain.

No one can look forward with complacency to a separation of the colony from the Mother Country brought about by a misunderstanding between them; apart even from sentiment, such an event would be an immense disaster. But if the yoke of political subjection galled till it was practically removed, we must expect that the yoke of diplomatic and commercial subjection, which has not been removed, will sometimes gall.

Nor, in regard to the internal constitution of our Dominion, is it likely that matters will long remain as they are. Sir Francis Hincks sets me down as bitterly hostile to Confederation because I hold that the measure did not go far enough and has consequently failed of its effect. The Provinces have not been blended into a united community; they remain separate interests, external in a great measure even to the Old Canadian parties, and make their separate terms with the party chiefs. Sectionalism, both of race and religion, is as strong and as noxious as ever; the conflict between Orangemen and Catholics has attained the character of a petty civil war, and Sir Francis Hincks himself speaks of the Scotch as a separate nationality, with special sentiments and exercising a special influence in our political affairs. I do not cast the blame on England. Some at least of the English statesmen who were engaged, and perhaps the English people generally believed, that Confederation was destined, at no distant period, to be crowned by nationality. Lord Derby, from his very want of originality, is always a good index of the prevailing tone of the time. That the functions of the Dominion Government are clearly defined by statute I have never denied; but what is in federations, the proper work of the federal government—the conduct of foreign affairs and the determination of all questions between the members of the federation—is, in the case of dependencies, reserved to the government of the Imperial country. The consequence is that the Dominion Government is without adequate objects, and the cost of a session at Ottawa, computed at $600,000, is ridiculously disproportioned to the amount of useful work done. To legislative union, at all events, we must come, if we are to be a united community independent of the American Republic. The mere expense of this galaxy of little constitutional monarchies with their separate parliaments and trappings, in the present state of our finances, will soon enforce a reconsideration of the existing arrangement.

Since the publication of his reply to me, Sir Francis Hincks has been engaged in a controversy with Sir Julius Vogel, lately Premier of New Zealand, on the subject of Imperial Federation. Sir Julius Vogel urgently recommends that measure, on the ground that for want of it the Colonial Empire is tending to dissolution, so that the confidence of this very competent judge in connexionist sentiment and the influences which tell in favour of the existing system is not so great as that of Sir Francis Hincks. Sir Julius seems to have caught the tone of British loyalty more successfully than that of British liberty. He appears to think the coercion of Cuba by Spain an example not unfit for England to follow towards British Colonies. Unwarned by the emblematic teaching of King Canute he proposes to arrest the tide of progress by an Act of Parliament, declaring that no British Colony shall ever become an independent nation. It is curious to consider what would have been the effect of such an Act had it been operative in the case of the United States. We should have had fifty millions, and in time a hundred millions, of English-speaking people without entire self-government, and perhaps with their capacity for it fatally impaired by the long habit of dependence; a giant in leading strings; a colossal baby among the nations; a frame of prodigious magnitude, but without a centre of thought or action in itself, and borrowing a languid animation from the heart and brain of a distant body. In place of American patriotism we should have had the worship of some British nobleman sent out as Governor-General; in place of national pride, restless and self-abasing efforts to attract the notice of the superior country; in place of the elevating ambition which looks to national gratitude for its reward, the ambition not so elevating which looks elsewhere. The United States in perpetual tutelage is the logical consequence of the principles held in common by Sir Julius Vogel and Sir Francis Hincks; but are they ready to embrace it? If not, they must admit that their loyalty, like mine, has rational bounds.

One word before I close, upon a subject which is partly personal but concerns others more than myself. In the paper on which I have been commenting, it is suggested, and in another paper it has been plainly stated that I have had some political object of my own in view; that I have attempted to form an Independence party with myself at the head of it, and that I have solicited the co-operation of members of the House of Commons, though in vain. This is the stuff of which a politician's dreams are made. I have never attempted to form a party of any kind, or solicited the co-operation of any member of the House of Commons in any plan or for any object whatever.

The National movement was the offspring, the inevitable offspring, of Confederation. It was fostered by the appeals of men who have since found it convenient not only to turn against it, but to brand it as sedition, and to hound down those who sympathized with it as traitors. In the essay of Professor Cairnes on Colonial Government, a speech of Mr. Brown is quoted as a proof that the public men of Canada were making no secret of their aspirations. Before I settled in Canada, the movement had been fully developed; it had put forth its manifesto in the form of the remarkable pamphlet entitled "Canada First;" it had given birth to a National Association, which I believe was originally composed of native Canadians, and of which I never was a member.

The stirrings of national life were felt as usual not only in the political but in the intellectual sphere. There was a desire for a national magazine, and as I had leisure and literary experience, the publishers enlisted me in the enterprise. It was at first determined, at my instance, that the magazine should be purely literary, and that politics should be excluded. From this determination it was found necessary to depart, in deference to the taste of the general public, and an article, non-party in its character, on Current Events was introduced. The measure of success achieved by the Canadian Monthly,* in face of the tremendous competition not only of the English magazines, but of the splendid periodical literature of the United States, shows the strength of the sentiment which gave it birth. That he has an organ in Canada for the discussion of a Canadian question, Sir Francis Hincks owes to the movement of which he speaks with contemptuous hatred, and which he and the politicians as a class have, not unnaturally, done their utmost to put down.

Of the founders of the weekly *Nation* I was not one; I was not in the country at the time. Looking to the circumstances of our country, and

---

* Let me take the opportunity as one of the founders of the Magazine of offering my best wishes to the spirited and patriotic publishers into whose hands it has lately passed.

the numbers of our reading public, I should hardly have been inclined to attempt the publication of a journal in so expensive and aristocratic a form. The programme, instead of embodying my special opinions on the Colonial question, contained a clause in favour of Imperial Federation. At a later period, I accepted an invitation to join the paper, because it was in the hands of my friends, and because I felt sure that it would be conducted honourably and with perfect independence. It sought, consistently I believe, to aid in raising the national spirit above mere colonialism, in giving national interests the ascendency over those of party, in maintaining decency of discussion, and in protecting the character of public men. Its success was great considering its form and the limited area of its circulation. I think I may say with truth that it was regarded by men even of opposite opinions as creditable to the Canadian press, and that it thus performed the proper duties of journalism, and fulfilled the legitimate objects of a journalist's ambition. It lent, if I mistake not, an impulse to the growing independence of our press, and when the loss of the principal writers, who were called away by other work, compelled us to suspend the publication, another independent journal sprang from the same root.

Sympathize with the national movement of course I did: in what should a political student and inquirer feel an interest, if not in a movement which promised to give birth to a nation? Sympathize with it I did, and heartily, but I left its political conduct to Canadians. I had turned fronf the gate of political life when it was opened to me in England, and I have never sought or desired to enter it here.* I have taken no active part in Canadian politics. A few days ago I attended for the first time a political meeting. My name would hardly have been heard in connection with public affairs if the rules and privileges of journalism had not been systematically violated in my person, with the design of driving from the Canadian press an independent journalist whose pen might infringe the monopoly of opinion which it was the object of the assailants, for their commercial as well as for their political purposes, to maintain. It was the independence of the Canadian press, not a political theory or

---

* Perhaps I ought to say that I was at one time inclined to entertain a proposal of bringing me forward for the Local House. It appeared to me that the Local House ought to be regarded as municipal rather than political, and there were some educational questions of importance which I might have taken up, there being then no Minister of Education; but I found party politics in my way, and at once gave up the idea.

scheme, that was attacked in my person. Err I very likely may from ignorance or misconception; but there is not a man in the Dominion to whom, individually, it matters less what course political events may take, than it does to me. In seconding, as far as I was able with propriety to second, the movement in favour of Canadian nationality, I was not actuated, so far as I am aware, by any selfish or sinister motive, but merely by a natural sympathy with an aspiration generous in itself, and in accordance with the views as to the general destinies of free British colonies which I had previously expressed; and I feel some satisfaction in thinking that I have not to bear even that small portion of blame which attaches to a private citizen, if nothing is now left as an ultimate mark for Canadian statesmanship but to prepare the terms of continental union.

OPINION

OF

LORD BLACHFORD,

Formerly Permanent Under-Secretary *for the Colonies,*

ON IMPERIAL FEDERATION

As the colonies develop they must either become separate nations, or they must have a share—eventually the greater share—in the government of the British Confederacy. Questions might arise on the working of the Federal Constitution. It does not appear whether the Imperial Ministry (which would include at least the foreign, colonial, and war ministers) is to be controlled and practically appointed by the Imperial Legislature or by the English Parliament; nor whether India and the Crown colonies are to be considered as Imperial or English property; nor whether the stimulus given to the establishment of responsible government in Ireland, Scotland, and Wales would be advantageous or otherwise; nor whether recent experience recommends a composite Legisature; nor whether it would be possible, with the requisite promptitude, to eradicate the sentimental objection which most Englishmen would feel to reducing the old historical House of Commons to the dimensions of a local legislature; nor whether it would be worth while for the colonies to send away for the greater part of every year so large a proportion of their leading men as would be necessary to secure a proper voting power in the Imperial Councils. But, all these queries notwithstanding, I am quite prepared to admit that the integrity of the British Empire could not be perpetuated by any rearrangement less objectionable than that which Sir Julius Vogel proposes. Indeed, I would add the observation that if, in the course of fifty years, such a metamorphosis became necessary, it might be found convenient, before the century was out, to consider whether the seat of government ought not to be at Melbourne rather than London. The relative position of Australia and India, added to the acquisitions of Oceania and New Guinea, certain to be effected under Australasian influence, appears to point to such a transfer, which by that time might be justified by the relative wealth and population of the different States of the Union. The question would be a very real one, and would have arisen before now with regard to New York, if it had been possible for us to retain our North American provinces till now.

I do not raise any quarrel upon these details, or pursue the thoughts which they suggest; I object to the conception out of which they arise. With "Empire" that conception has nothing to do. The Imperial relation only subsists in substance between the United Kingdom on the one hand and India and the Crown colonies on the other. It subsists in form and in form only between the United Kingdom and the constitutional colonies. For that formal and delusive relation of empire it is proposed, by steps, which, if they are taken at all, must be taken in no long time—say in the course of the next half century—to substitute a real working confederacy. The conception is that of a close and permanent association between self-governed States, not arising out of geographical neighbourhood. To this conception I object as hollow and impracticable.

Every association of human beings must have a purpose, and the object of every association must be to combine in employing means for the attainment of that purpose, according to some understood rules. Men associate for comfort or pleasure, and become a club; for gain, and be-

THE POLITICAL DESTINY OF CANADA. 173

come a company; to return a member of Parliament, and become a committee; for the advancement of art or science, and become a society; for the all-embracing purpose of securing order, prosperity, and safety in the territory which they occupy, and become a State.

The proposed Confederation will be an association. What is its common purpose? Evidently to secure and further the order, prosperity, and safety of the Confederation, so far as these are to be secured and furthered by the action of a common and supreme authority. But in what sense is this a common purpose? A common aspiration it no doubt is. But a common purpose, capable of being made the principle of a confederacy, must be something which can be pursued by common efforts and a common policy. Of what common efforts and common policy will the proposed confederacy be capable? What is that sphere of combined action which is a condition of its real existence?

I understand alliances and treaties between independent powers, for specific purposes. I even understand what is in form a general defensive and offensive alliance, if it is, at bottom, based on some such specific and terminable purpose. But a confederacy affects a much closer solidarity; it aims at securing that, within certain limits, but under all sorts of unforeseen circumstances, the interests, and quarrels, and responsibilities of each part shall be the interests, and quarrels, and responsibilities of the whole. What are these limits? What are to be the functions of the confederacy as such with respect to these interests and responsibilities?

The supreme power of a confederacy may deal either with the purely internal affairs of its component members, or with their relations to each other, or with their foreign policy.

With the first of these it is fully admitted that the intended confederacy will have nothing whatever to do. This immense department of law and government must be exclusively and jealously and properly reserved to the State authorities. The effect of this reservation in confining the functions of the central power will at once be felt if we remember how small a proportion of the legislative and administrative action of our own country relates to anything but the internal affairs of the United Kingdom.

Next come what may be called inter-provincial questions. Such, it may be said, are customs duties, ocean postage, immigration, the treatment of offences committed at sea, extradition, alienage, slavery, the treatment of natives, the machinery of common defence, and others, possibly which do not occur to me. Each of these has called for consideration in its day, and some have presented great difficulty. But much has settled itself. Events have determined that, in respect to self-governed colonies, some of these, like customs duties and immigration, must be treated as internal. About others, like alienage, extradition, and the treatment of offences committed on the high seas, arrangements may be necessary, as with foreign countries, but no serious difficulty need be anticipated. Others are definitively settled by an accepted Imperial law, like slavery; others narrowed geographically by the course of events, like the treatment of natives. Some will remain the subject of what may be called administrative negotiation, like ocean postage and (I should say) the machinery of common defence. Great questions in this department can at present scarcely be said to exist, while small ones are generally matters of discussion between the home Government and one or more of the colonies. It is perhaps worth while to explain the mode in which such discussions are now conducted. They are conducted through the governor, through whom all authoritative communications pass, and whose advice the home Government expects in all matters to receive; but whose reports are supplemented by concurrent explanations received less authoritatively from the accredited agents of the different colonial Governments, who have full cognisance of the views of their respective Governments, free access to the Colonial Office, and full opportunities for acting in concert on any question in which any number of colonies have a common interest. This method is probably not without some inconvenience. No method is likely to be otherwise which involves negotiations of detail—sometimes in the nature of bargains—between authorities at opposite ends of the earth. But it is, after all, not very inappropriate to the work which has to be done; it is capable of adjustment to meet discovered inconveniences or altering circumstances; and I am not aware of any reason for supposing that colonial Governments would prefer to it either Sir Julius Vogel's immediate proposal of a representative Council of Advice, which, if it is to have the power of controlling the Government of England, should also have that of binding those of the colonies, or the prospect of a Confederate Legislature, which would settle questions over their heads, and whose conclusions, if they happened to be carried by English votes, would not be always well received. Assuming, however, that some two or three questions of this class would be more satisfactorily settled by a representative central authority than hammered out by piecemeal negotiation, I contend that their aggregate and decreasing bulk is plainly insufficient to strengthen materially the *raison d'être* for a Confederate Legislature.

It remains that this *raison d'être* must be found, if anywhere, in foreign politics. And here it appears to me, the conception completely breaks down. To such a confederacy as we are imagining foreign politics may be supposed to supply a sphere of action, only till we remember that it does not supply a common purpose. For, in relation to foreign politics, what purposes are common to England and her colonies as a mass? In the course of the last thirty years we have had wars in China, India, and Abyssinia, some or other of us have talked of war with the United States in aid of the Secessionists, of war with Austria and Prussia on behalf of Denmark, of war with Germany in aid of France, and now of war with Russia on behalf of British interests in or about Turkey. In which of these questions have the colonies any interest? If any such question involves us in a maritime war, they will no doubt suffer, but **their interest** in that case will not be **in the object of the war,** but in the war itself. It will be a simple interest of suffering. **We may fairly** enough say to them as the whole Empire may at **any** moment be called on to put itself **into** peril for their protection, so **they must be** content to suffer inconvenience when the Empire **goes to** war for its own objects. But we cannot allege that **they will be suffering for** any object of their own or in support of a policy **from** which they will derive any **benefit.** What **have they to** do with the command **of the Mediterranean,** or the road **to** India, **or the** balance **of power, or the** invasion **of Belgium?** One of **them** is interested in the **cod** fisheries of the Atlantic, another in the development of Oceania or **the annexation of New** Guinea, another in the pacification of Central Africa—objects all which have to be considered between Great Britain and the particular colony concerned, because in each **case we** are responsible for asserting the rights of **those** who depend upon **us. But in** the external **war policy of the** Empire **as such** no colony has any tangible share, **except in so far as they** may suffer from **a state of war.** No doubt their influence in our councils would, *exceptis excipiendis*, be pacific, and this is so far good. But is it yet right that the councils of any great nation should be weighted with au element which is steadily against war, without having an interest in those objects for which war may become imperatively necessary? I admit that in some commercial matters confederation might facilitate the conduct of negotiations with foreign Powers, who cannot understand colonial independence. But this would be at the cost of enabling the colonies to obstruct, in its application to foreign countries, the principle of free trade, or any other on which England may consider her commercial prosperity to depend.

Is it possible to expect that any great Power will consent to be so weighted? Rather is it not certain that, in the absence of any prevailing purpose and consolidating bias, each member of the confederacy, finding itself unable to carry its peculiar objects, will, sooner or later, think itself ill-treated, and claim the right of taking care of itself? Can this tendency be resisted? It can only be resisted, as Sir Julius Vogel plainly proposes to resist it—by force. If force is not to be applied, the result must be that so long as the advantages of following in the train of a great nation appear to outweigh the damage and peril

—or rather, for sentiment's sake, somewhat longer—these communities will remain willingly attached to Great Britain. When the connection becomes a grievance, they will disengage themselves. If I were compelled to hazard a prophecy, I should guess that our great colonies would endure manfully the inconveniences of one great war, but would shrink from the prospect of a second. But, whatever the vitality of our present relations, there is between us, I contend, no such common purpose or group of purposes as will give us a common desire to pursue a common policy. And without this I see no basis for a union between practically independent powers.

The conclusion of the whole seems to me one which it is easier to dislike than to disprove. Our present relations with our grown-up colonies are exceedingly satisfactory, and the longer they continue the better. But there is a period in the life of distant nations, however close their original connection, at which each must pursue its own course, whether in domestic or foreign politics, unembarrassed by the other's leading. And the arrival of that period depends upon growth. Every increase of colonial wealth, or numbers, or intelligence, or organisation, is in one sense a step towards disintegration. The Confederation of

Canada was therefore such a step. The Confederation of South Africa will be, in the same sense, another. All these are steps of a wholesome kind, which only facilitate separation by providing againts its evils; and it is hardly a paradox to say that they may delay it by preparing for it. An agreeable but transitory relation is often prolonged by the sense that when it becomes irksome it can be terminated without difficulty. On the other hand if it is seriously believed possible that nations internally independent, and externally divided by oceans, like England, Canada, South Africa, and Australasia, can remain for ever united in one political system for the sole purpose of determining a foreign policy in which no three of them have a common object; and if English statesmen seriously undertake to render a union under such conditions perpetual, it is to be apprehended that, in their struggles against dismemberment, they may either attempt, by a sacrifice of "British interests," to bribe the colonies into a cohesion which cannot really be secured, or may alienate them by showing a suspicious disinclination to recognise that national manhood into which they are rapidly rising—a grudging desire to withhold what may enable them to stand by themselves. I only add, by way of illustration, that Sir Julius's reference to the value of colonial loans on the Stock Exchange, and to the effect of a closer connection in increasing that value, suggests a passing apprehension lest, among other things, of the phrase " confederation " may be begotten the substance " guarantee."

For these reasons I ask those who are most keenly set on maintaining the integrity of the Empire to examine accurately what is the meaning of these words, not, of course, with regard to India and the Crown colonies, in respect to which England really possesses Imperial powers and duties, but as to the constitutional colonies which govern themselves.

—*From the Nineteenth Century.*

OPINION

OF THE

RIGHT HON. ROBERT LOWE, M.P.,

ON THE

VALUE TO THE UNITED KINGDOM

OF THE

COLONIAL DOMINIONS OF THE CROWN.

In ancient times the value of a territorial acquisition to the country that obtained it was a very simple affair. The colonies of Greece were considered by the parent state mainly in the light of outlets for the redundant population of a poor and mountainous country. The colonies of Rome were planted almost entirely for military purposes, and, if they answered these, nothing else was demanded from them. But as regards territories acquired by conquest or by cession the case was very different. After undergoing a spoliation more or less complete they settled down into a miserable and abject dependence, a tribute was wrung from them regulated rather by the greed of the exactors than by the ability of the tributaries, and the choicest of their youth were enrolled in the armies of their cruel and rapacious conquerors. The measure of the value of such an acquisition was just what could be wrung from it in men and money without destroying its power of further contribution. The Spaniards did not even observe this rule. In their greed for gold they exterminated the natives of Hispaniola in working the mines, and were thus driven to the humane suggestion of Las Casas, the importation of Africans to supply the race which they had murdered. The value of these acquisitions was therefore the realised property and the labour of the race, whether extorted from them in the character of slaves or tributaries. From this sum there was very little deduction for the expense of government. A few magistrates exercising indiscriminately executive and judicial functions without diligence and without appeal or revision, sufficed for the government of such a society, which may be best described as a state of collective slavery. Whatever may be thought of the morality of such a proceeding, we cannot wonder that the acquisition of a state to be held on such terms was regarded as a source of wealth to the conquerors. What we seek to discover is, what in the absence of all these cruel and unjust means of acquisition, and after allowing for the expense of a thoroughly efficient and good government, is the value to the paramount state of a foreign dependency. We are not aware that such an inquiry has ever been attempted, nor can we regard it as a mere matter of curiosity. Occasions are continually arising when it is of the utmost importance to know accurately the worth of the interests with which we have to deal, and the statesman can no more dispense with this knowledge than the trader can deal with wares of which he has not ascertained the value.

The foreign dominions of the Crown may be divided for the purposes of this inquiry into three parts. 1. Places which are held for purely naval and military purposes, such as Gibraltar and Malta. 2. Those which are more or less fitted to be the residence of English labour, such as Canada, the southern parts of Australia, the Cape, Tasmania, and New Zealand. 3. Those whose climate renders it impossible that they should ever become the residence of a labouring population composed of persons of European descent, such as India, the West Indian Islands and the northern parts of Australia. The value of the first division is a matter purely for soldiers and sailors—our concern is with the two last alone. If this inquiry had been made a hundred years ago, there can be no doubt as to the answer that would have been given. In the absence of any actual experience on the subject, it was then universally believed that the loss of the American colonies was a fatal blow from which the nation could never recover. Of course this was in some degree owing to the mistaken views which were then entertained as to the value of the monopoly of the colonial trade. But even when allowance has been made for this exploded error, there still remains a great amount of terror and despondency which we now know to have been utterly groundless, and which can only be accounted for by a gross mistake of words for things. The Englishman of a hundred years ago believed, as we believe at the present day, that the elements which constitute the indispensable conditions of the greatness of a State are inhabitants, territory, and capital. He saw that the American Revolution deprived us, as far as America was concerned, of all three, and he looked no farther. Had he dived a little deeper into the matter, he would have seen that the value of all these things depends entirely on the degree in which they can be made useful to the State which is the nominal owner of them.

Now, as to the territory, it is quite clear that its loss is a very inconsiderable evil so long as it is (as is the case with all civilized nations) just as accessible to us as if it was our own. The United States, since their separation from us, have received far more British emigrants from us than our remaining colonies. Our people have settled and thriven on the land that they are said to have lost in North America.

Then as to the inhabitants. The English Crown lost three millions of thriving and industrious subjects; but then the question arises, Did the English Crown ever possess them in the sense which could make their loss a serious misfortune? Why are the subjects a support to the State? Because the wealth which they possess is a fund from which the State can draw, and on which it can borrow for the supply of its necessities. Subjects are also a support to a State, because they are the natural defenders to whom it looks in war for protection. We venture to suggest that the reason why the loss of the American colonies was so little felt by those who expected to feel it so deeply was, that the colonists of North America had never, or only in a very slight degree, felt or discharged either of these duties. They never assisted us in our wars in

Europe or anywhere except where they themselves were concerned, and so little idea had they of aiding us with money, that they separated from us rather than contribute to our revenue. They never performed towards us the duties of full citizenship, and reason as well as experience shows that we could not be injured by the withdrawal of services which we never enjoyed. But this is not all. A country may incur very heavy liabilities on account of subjects who make her no return. Our Consuls in the East could tell us of the great relief which they would experience, if the Maltese, for instance, were not as much entitled to the protection of the British power as the inhabitants of London. Subjects are not always a support, but they very often become a burden. We spent ten millions in order to rescue from captivity three or four British subjects detained in Abyssinia, and we did this mainly to keep up our influence in India, which did not give a man or a rupee for the service. We do not put forward these considerations as showing that there are not many advantages in a colonial empire such as we now hold, and may, we trust, long continue to hold. The close union that still exists between us and our present colonial dominions is highly honourable to both parties, and has an obvious **tendency to** promote trade **and** cement friendship. But it is idle to attempt **to** conceal from ourselves that this union is in **its** very nature temporary and precarious, and **may,** and probably will, be put **an** end to without **any** misconduct on either side.

In the first place the union **is** one-sided. In **case** of war we are bound to defend Canada and Australia just as **much as we are bound to defend** Great Britain and **Ireland.** But there is **no** reciprocal obligation. **The** colonies do all that **we** require, and more than we expect, if they defend themselves. The cause of war is almost sure **to be one in which** all, or at any rate **many, of the colonies** have no interest. They **will** naturally **feel** regret that they are exposed **to loss** and injury in a cause which **is not theirs, and we** ought **not** to blame them if they **prefer their own** interests to **ours. The present is** essentially a fair-weather **plan. Like Don** Quixote's Helmet, it has broken down once, and we shall do wisely **not** to be too confident in it for the future.

It is besides not likely that the Colonies will ultimately be content without having a voice in those deliberations by which their **welfare** may be so seriously affected. To gratify this reasonable desire would amount to a remodelling **of** Parlia-

ment on a federal principle. To this there are two insuperable objections: one the impossibility of persuading England and Scotland, and perhaps even Ireland, to consent to such a change; the other the difficulty which is sure to arise among the colonies themselves. * * * *
On the second point, which has hitherto escaped observation, we will offer a few remarks.

Every colony is, by the ties of Government, trade, and a certain degree of common interest, connected with the Imperial Government. The colony looks back to her origin and her history, inseparably intertwined with our own.

> "And Rome may bear the pride of him of whom herself is proud."

Much may and doubtless would be conceded to the mother-country which would be conceded to no one else; with her there is no spirit of rivalry. But of an assembly composed partly of representatives of the mother-country and partly of the representatives of other colonies, each colony would be utterly intolerant. They would say, and with some justice, that they recognize the right of England to a voice in matters affecting their welfare, but that they utterly deny the right of any one colony to exercise any influence over the affairs of another.

Every one whose lot it has been to be practically acquainted with the sentiments and aspirations of a colonial community, is well aware that one colony seldom errs on the side of over-estimating the advantages or good qualities of its neighbour. They are apt to regard each other more as rivals than as co-operators. The products of those that lie near each other are mostly similar, and they are competitors for custom in the London market. Many reasons may be given why it would be very much for the interest of the Australian colonies to form a confederacy somewhat on the pattern of the United States, or at least to join in a Zollverein, and thus save the expense and delay of inter-colonial custom-houses. But though no one can deny this in the abstract, these reasons have hitherto been urged in vain. There is but one really efficacious motive to draw them into a confederacy, and that motive is fear. Where that is present the thing may be forced upon the colonies, as in North America and South Africa; where this is wanting, as in Australia, minor inducements are tried in vain.

But if this repulsion exists so strongly between neighbouring colonies, what will it be between colonies separated from each other by the diameter of the earth? Will Canada accept laws from New Zealand ? or Australia submit to the legislation of Jamaica ? And yet the only conceivable scheme by which the colonies can possibly be admitted to share in imperial councils is an assembly in which the Crown and the colonies shall be alike represented.

Whenever, therefore, the time shall arrive for the colonies to claim a voice in the general policy of the empire, there is nothing for it but separation, since the only alternative that can be suggested is utterly unworkable. The result is, that we shall act most wisely by looking the question fairly in the face, whenever the inevitable day shall arrive when our larger colonies shall make the claim to have a voice in imperial affairs, and solve the question by submitting patiently and graciously to the inevitable alternative of separation, instead of exaggerating the mischief by futile efforts to avert it. It is not natural that nations which are destined, probably in the lifetime of some persons now in existence, to become more numerous than our own, should submit to be for ever in a state of tutelage. Our wisdom is to defer the change as long as possible, and when it does come, to throw no captious obstacles in the way, but to console ourselves by the reflection that the experience of a hundred years ago shows us that it is very easy to exaggerate the mischiefs that arise from such a separation; above all, we should be on our guard against such phrases as "the decline of the empire," the "setting of the sun of England," and other poetical and rhetorical expressions, which have really no application to a change that only marks an inevitable period in a singularly wise and beneficent policy of which we have every reason to be proud.

To those who view the probable separation of the colonies from the mother-country at some period more or less remote as a proof of our degeneracy as compared with those who founded them, it may be some consolation to observe that hardly any of these settlements at the present day are answering the purposes with which they were founded. The great object in founding a colony was undoubtedly to secure the monopoly of its trade, and so long as we confined ourselves to that the American Colonies were among the most loyal of our fellow-subjects. Australia was originally occupied as a penal settlement. The West India Islands were desired as fields for the employment of slave-labour; and India, as we shall see presently, was acquired for objects very different from those which are now assigned for its retention.

There remains for consideration the third and by far the most important part of our inquiry, the question, namely, of the amount of injury which we should sustain by the loss of those dominions of the Crown, which, being situated within the tropics or in their vicinity, can never become the home of a laborious and quickly multiplying European population. Our sugar islands were acquired as labour-fields for slaves, and with emancipation they lost the greater part of their value. Nature is so bountiful and life so easy in these lovely isles, and indolence so irresistible, that we lose greatly instead of gaining by the change from slave labour to free. To add to the depression in these once flourishing possessions, it pleases the Government of France, in addition to one hundred and nine millions which the nation has to pay for Government and the interest of debt, to raise another million, which is employed in bounties to enable the beetroot sugar of France to undersell the sugar of the tropics. No one, we think, will say that any considerable loss would be sustained if these islands were separated from the British dominions. There can, in fact, be no reason for retaining them except the honourable feeling that it would be disgraceful to England to allow some of the fairest spots of the earth to relapse into utter sloth, ignorance, and barbarism, after she has once taken them into her hands.

We now believe ourselves to be in a condition to answer the question which we proposed as to the value to the United Kingdom of the foreign dominions of the Crown other than military posts. The answer seems to be that to over-estimate it is extremely easy, and to under-estimate it extremely difficult. Having considerable faith in the soundness of opinions which are very generally entertained, we have done our best to find some ground for the belief that the colonies are the mainstay of the empire, and that we have in India the secret of our greatness, our wealth and our power. As will be seen, in this attempt we have utterly failed. The matter was extremely simple while we confined ourselves to vague generalities. As long as we limited our view to tables of imports and exports, to returns of population and numbers of square miles, the case seemed plain enough; but when we came to examine the relations in which the owners of these things stood to England, the scales fell from our eyes, and we saw that all these good things which we are instructed to regard as elements of our strength, were really ours in words alone; and what we were instructed to rely on as our own property turned out to be nothing better than a mere rhetorical flourish, in fact the property of others.

The question is not whether all these magnificent territories and swarming millions exist; nor yet whether they are set down in books of geography and gazetteers as forming part of the dominions of the British Crown; nor yet whether they are the objects of admiration to the nations of the earth. The question with which we, as practical people, are concerned is much simpler, and may be thus expressed. What is the relation in which the inhabitant of the British Isles stands to these possessions? Are they his in the same sense in which the wealth, the population, and the strength of the United Kingdom are his? The answer must be, that they are not. And if the question be further pressed, in what respect do they differ? The answer must be: The difference is simply this, that while we are bound to defend these vast possessions beyond the United Kingdom to our last shilling and our last man, the persons to whom we are so bound recognise no corresponding obligation, and after enjoying the fruits of our power and prosperity are at liberty to part from us, if they so think **fit,** in the moment of danger and distress. And, further, the answer must be that these dominions, which we call ours, give us no strength in war, and no funds at any time towards the support of our Government, and have been in the past the fruitful causes of wars.

We look for a solid repast, and can find nothing but a banquet of the Barmecide.

—*Fortnightly Review.*

www.ingramcontent.com/pod-product-compliance
Lightning Source LLC
Chambersburg PA
CBHW021734220426

43662CB00008B/846